Why Men Marry Some Women and Not Others

Also by John T. Molloy

New Women's Dress for Success

New Dress for Success

WHY MEN
MARRY
SOME WOMEN
AND NOT OTHERS

*The Fascinating Research
That can Land You the
Husband of Your Dreams*

JOHN T. MOLLOY

WARNER BOOKS

An AOL Time Warner Company

Warner Books, Inc., 1271 Avenue of the Americas, New York, NY 10020
Visit our Web site at www.twbookmark.com.

 An AOL Time Warner Company

Printed in the United States of America

First Printing: September 2003
10   9   8   7   6   5   4   3   2   1

The Library of Congress Cataloging-in-Publication Data

Molloy, John T.
    Why men marry some women and not others : the fascinating
research that can land you the husband of your dreams /
John T. Molloy.
        p.   cm.
    ISBN 0-446-53113-8
        1. Husbands.   2. Mate selection.   3. Man-woman relationships.
    4. Marriage.   I. Title.
    HQ756.M643   2003
    646.7'7—dc21

                                                    2003043285

This book, along with everything else I do,

is dedicated to Maureen and Rob

I would like to thank the half dozen or so women who started me researching marriage and the hundreds who would not let me quit. I am also grateful to the thousands who answered our questions, particularly the couples coming out of marriage license bureaus who postponed their celebrations and talked to my researchers. Without them I would not have the data on which this book is based. Finally, I am most grateful to Valerie Marz, Judy Stein, and John Aherne, whose skill helped me deliver this information in a clear and entertaining style.

Contents

Introduction

Any single woman who lets the research in this book be her guide has not only a better chance of marrying, but also a better chance of marrying the man she truly desires. I personally oversaw the studies on which the text is based and used the same team that has been conducting dress, image, and sales research for Fortune 500 corporations and government agencies, both here and abroad, for more than forty years.

This book is not a set of rules on how to manipulate a man into marriage. Rather, it's designed to provide women with valid statistical information that will help them make intelligent decisions in their search for that special man.

The first reason I believe this book will help women looking to switch their status from single to married is that its conclusions are based on thorough research. We interviewed, among others, 2,543 women and their fiancés coming out of marriage license bureaus, as well as 221 women in their late thirties and 463 in their forties who had no immediate prospects of marriage. We found that these two groups of women had different attitudes toward love, marriage, and life. We also discovered that unmarried women over forty had treated the men in their lives in a markedly different manner than the women who married in their twenties and early thirties. In addition, we sought information from some specific groups: men who went with one woman for years and immediately after breaking up with her married another; women who let others talk them out of marrying; men who had long-term relationships with one woman after another but never married; men who thought of themselves as confirmed bachelors; and so forth. Naturally, we ran focus groups anytime our interviews left questions unanswered or raised additional questions.

The second reason I believe this book will help women marry is that, during the last eleven years, between three hundred and four hundred single female researchers worked on the project or became familiar with the research, and more than half of them married within three years. Since 19 percent of these women were in their late thirties or early forties and many had virtually given up on the idea of marrying, this is an extraordinarily high number.

Finally, many of the very intelligent women who worked on the project believed the research helped them. I know, because scores of them thanked me personally and/or invited me to their weddings.

How the Project Began

The study was born in the late 1980s when Robin, a researcher I had hired to help me with a survey for a San Francisco firm, called and told me she could not show up the next day. She was calling from her older sister's place. As it happened, I knew Robin's sister, Kelly; she had worked for me as a researcher a few years earlier. Apparently, Kelly had just found out that a man she had dated for almost three years and broken up with five months earlier was marrying another woman. Robin said Kelly was so upset she couldn't leave her and even hinted that Kelly might be suicidal. Then she added, "It's partially your fault." Of course, I asked how it could be *my* fault.

Robin told me it wasn't the first time this had happened to her sister. Kelly had gone out with another man for two years, and a year after he had broken up with her, he had married someone else. While Kelly was working for me as a researcher, Robin reminded me, I had said over and over: *If an event repeats itself, there's usually a reason for it.* Then without another word, Robin hung up.

I was very upset that something I had said could make a person feel suicidal. No matter how innocuous the statement or how innocent my purpose had been, I felt pangs of guilt. Luckily, twenty minutes later the phone rang again. It was Kelly. Not only would Robin work the next morning, she said, but she herself would be willing to help. Then she added, "In return, I'd like you to do me a favor." Kelly wanted me to spend the afternoon with her, she said, to help her develop a research project that would show her what she was doing wrong with men she dated. The two men had treated her in an identical way, and she was convinced I had been right—there was a reason. She didn't want to turn off every man she met by making the same mistake she had made with those two.

I didn't know if I could come up with a study that would uncover such personal information, but she said all she asked was that I do my best. When I continued to hesitate, Robin got on the phone and pleaded with me to help. Reluctantly, I agreed. I knew Kelly was a very good researcher, and I was confident that if I developed a survey, she had the skills to use it effectively.

The next day, I told them the plan I'd hatched after getting off the phone with them the previous evening. Since Kelly wanted to know why two men she'd dated had married someone else, my plan was to stop couples coming out of the marriage license bureau and ask them about their relationships. That would let us compare her relationships to their relationships and see if there were any significant differences.

Kelly loved my idea, and we went to work. A majority of the engaged couples were young, in a good mood, and more than willing to talk about how, when, and where they had met and courted. First we asked general questions about their relationships; then we became more specific. The first step we took was to separate the men from the women, because, as experienced researchers, we knew both parties' answers would be more open and honest if the future spouse was not listening. We found a local diner and paid the owner to let us use the back room. I took the men to one table, and the two sisters took the women to another. We supplied refreshments and did our best to make them feel comfortable and relaxed.

After talking with the first three couples, we compared notes and added questions that would fill in gaps in our information. We quickly approached two more couples and interviewed them in the same place. This time, we tailored our questions to cover specific topics we thought needed further investigation. Before the marriage license bureau closed, we had questioned four sets of three or more couples, refining our approach after each set.

By the end of the day, Kelly reported that she knew exactly what she was doing wrong with the men she dated. I sat her down and told her she was too good a researcher to say that. We had interviewed only fourteen people each, and there was no way data from such a small sample could answer a question as complex as the one she had raised. Nevertheless, Kelly declared, she knew the answer: "My mistake was that *I* was not committed enough to marriage to insist on it."

She saw the irony of her statement. She went on to observe that women like to accuse men of not being able to commit, but some of those same women aren't committed enough to getting married to demand that their boyfriends marry them.

During her last two sets of interviews, without letting me know, Kelly had asked a new question: "If on your way to the marriage license bureau, your man had turned to you and said, 'I'm not ready,' or 'I just can't see myself as a married man,' or something similar, what would you have done?" As she was driving with her first fiancé to get their marriage license, Kelly told me, he had announced he was not ready for marriage and turned the car around. She'd agreed to give him time, and she was now convinced she had made a mistake.

Sixty percent of the women coming out of marriage license bureaus she interviewed that day (and, as it turned out, more than 60 percent of the women we were to interview over the next ten years) gave essentially the same answer. They would give their intended an ultimatum: Marry me, *or else.*

Their answers were not identical in content or tone. A number of the women said they would give him an ultimatum the instant the question was raised, but most only hinted that they would leave him. Bear in mind, these were women who had just picked up a marriage license with the man of their dreams. Most could not bring themselves to say they would dump him. A majority said they would talk to their fiancé and help him get over his nerves. The women assumed their fiancés would just be suffering from a case of the prenuptial jitters. Their answers were generally more conciliatory than "I'd get rid of him." When the question was refined, however, to stipulate that no matter what they did or said, he maintained he was not ready for marriage and didn't know when or if he ever would be, nearly 60 percent indicated that they would break up with him. Most added, by way of explanation, that they would not let these men ruin their lives.

Kelly understood that interviewing a handful of couples really didn't give her a statistically meaningful answer. But she assured me that she was willing to interview as many couples as it took to develop one. Kelly, Robin, and I spent several hours at an airport restaurant as I waited for my flight, fleshing out a survey that would identify the differences between relationships that led to marriage and those that did not.

I took a copy of the survey with me to polish on the plane. After I got home, we spent two hours on the telephone putting together a questionnaire and working out interviewing procedures. I agreed that when Kelly sent me the raw data, I would write a report.

After a month or two, I stopped watching my mail for the results of the survey. I figured Kelly had given up on the project, since she thought she had already found the answer she needed. Six months later, when UPS delivered an enormous box of papers, I was flabbergasted. She had questioned not only people coming out of the San Francisco marriage license bureau but also newly married couples, as well as twenty-three men who had serious relationships with one woman but married another shortly after breaking off with the first. Kelly had expanded the research, and although she'd made a few mistakes in approach, most of her information was valid.

Because I had to redo one of the focus groups and survey 140 engaged couples myself, it took me almost five months to put together the report. When I shipped it off to Kelly, I thanked her for the agreement she had sent giving me exclusive rights to the research. I'm sure it was a carrot to get me to spend time fine-tuning and analyzing the material. Nevertheless, I included with the report the standard nondisclosure agreement I have all my researchers sign, even though at the time I had no intention of using the material to write a book. The commitment I had made on the spur of the moment had cost me so much time and money that I didn't want to look at that research ever again.

The First to Test the Research

Almost two years to the day after Kelly had started the research, she called to tell me she was getting married. She had followed the guidance she had gleaned from her own research. She had found a new man she was crazy about, but she had not let him treat her the way the first two men did. Kelly also reported that her sister, Robin, had just become engaged, and she thought the reason she had no problem getting her boyfriend to commit was that she had also used my report as her guide. That was nine years ago.

In October 1993, the next stage of the research had its beginning when another young woman, Karen, confronted me in the hallway of a company where I was running training sessions in nonverbal sales techniques. She complained that my report on getting married—which was being passed around without my permission—did not answer all the questions she had. Karen indignantly pointed out that, according to the report, there's a certain time in most relationships when men are most likely to commit—but the report never explained when that occurs. She was outraged that I thought there were stages in relationships but had not bothered to identify them. "Don't you think you have an obligation to find out?" she demanded.

This irate young woman also wanted to know if, after several dates, a bright woman could tell if a man was a prospective husband or an immature clown. When Karen paused for breath, I asked her if she had a copy of the report. Without missing a beat, she pulled one from her purse. I explained that the report was only a research summary, hoping this would get her to back off. Instead, Karen asked if I would design a survey to answer her questions. I had her sign the agreements necessary if I ever wanted to include the research in a book, but the real reason I went along with her proposal was that she was one of my star pupils in the sales course, and I wanted to keep her happy.

I promised to develop the survey on three conditions. First, only the people who attended my sales sessions could conduct the survey. Second, she and her friends could not talk about what we were doing. Third, the research procedure must be followed exactly as designed, and no one could make changes without my permission. She immediately agreed to all my conditions, and I designed a small survey that would answer most of her questions. I agreed, as I had with Kelly, that after she finished the project, I would take the raw data and summarize it.

A couple of months later, this second group turned in their survey results. Not trained researchers, they hadn't done as good a job as Kelly's group; in fact, some of their questioning was rather sloppy. Nevertheless, they had come up with some interesting information. When I combined their data with the first study, it turned out to be one of those times when one plus one added up to more than two. The research also raised more questions than it answered, but I still never thought it would become a book.

Once word got out that I had such a report, almost every unmarried woman who worked for me and hundreds of their friends asked to read it. Some even reviewed the raw data. At least thirty groups of female researchers volunteered to conduct additional surveys if I would analyze the data they collected. I refused all but two of these offers, because I began to see a potential book and knew I had to control all future research. I spent three months in the field developing the final version of the marriage license bureau surveys.

I was aware of the "rose-colored-glasses" effect and considered it when interpreting the data. When interviewing couples who'd just picked up marriage licenses, asking them to describe the person with whom they intended to spend the rest of their lives, I expected their descriptions to be unrealistic. If there was any moment in their lives when they were going to look at their mates through rose-colored glasses, this would be it. It's the old "I-bought-it" factor. If you ask people shopping for their first minivan which one is the best on the market, most will say they aren't sure. Even those who have decided which minivan they intend to buy are likely to qualify their answers. But if you ask the same respondents the same question after they have just purchased a van, most will tell you the one they own is the best.

Concluding the Research

I took over the research in 1994 and developed several versions of the survey to look at different aspects of the subject. After that, I spent several hours in front of marriage license bureaus questioning people in every area I visited. The nature of some research makes the skill and experience of the researcher very important, so from that point on, I used only experienced researchers or conducted the research myself.

Questions about sex, for example, really demand using only experienced researchers. In addition, we found that older researchers of the same gender elicited far more open and honest responses than younger ones, so we used older researchers when discussing sex. Whenever possible, I personally led focus groups, because I can get more information out of them than anyone who works for me. My people and I worked on this until June 2000.

Six Findings on the Path to Marrying Men

The first thing we learned from the research was that Kelly's early conclusion was right on target. The primary difference between women who marry and those who do not is this:

Women who marry insist on marriage. They settle for nothing else.

The second thing we learned is:

Women who married were far less likely to have wasted their time in dead-end relationships.

Many of them told us they'd had previous relationships that were serious but broke them off because they were going nowhere.

Third:

Women who married loved themselves more than they loved any man.

You can best understand their thinking if you examine why a majority of them referred to the men they dropped as "losers." At first I thought they meant the men were failures in business or socially, but that was not the case.

The reason most of these women thought of their former boyfriends as losers was that these men would not commit, and as a result did not meet the women's needs.

Fourth, this study showed that:

Women who are committed to the idea of marriage are much more likely to marry than those who are not.

There is no question some women marry because they are beautiful, lucky, or charming. They meet a man they like who is crazy about them and cannot wait to marry them. Without much commitment or effort, they walk down the aisle. In most cases, however, marriage is a result of women putting pressure, sometimes subtle and sometimes not so subtle, on the men who marry them.

Which leads to the fifth statistical truth:

Women who are slender have an easier time meeting men and better odds of getting married.

The women getting their marriage licenses were more slender than the women who were single. By keeping yourself in shape and your appearance up, you're more likely to attract men. And let's face it, you have to attract a man before you can get close enough to him to determine whether he is marriage material.

The sixth major finding is:

Time is the single woman's enemy.

To be on the safe side, a woman should start seriously looking for a husband in her late twenties. Assume it takes a couple of years to find out if a man is *the* man. If he's not, a woman in her late twenties still has the mobility of the singles scene. She increases her chances dramatically over starting to look at age thirty-one, because it gives her several more years in the singles scene.

Naturally, there are men available at any age, but the pool of men shrinks with time, and it becomes more difficult to meet them.

Like most pop science writers, I try to explain complicated data in relatively simple terms. I am happiest when the information lends itself to listing rules or commandments: Do A, B, C, and D, but do not do E, F, G, or H; wear A, B, C, and D, but never wear E, F, G, or H. Because we are dealing with very complex relationships, this study produced few if any absolute truths. As a result, I have no unbreakable rules or commandments to offer. Instead, at the end of each chapter I list guidelines based on the statistical findings that are designed to increase your odds of marrying.

With the information this book will give you, you can arrange the odds in your favor at any age. Relationships between men and women are too complex to make guarantees, but if you'd like to have the odds on your side in your personal battle of the sexes, read on.

Guidelines for Marrying Men Based on Six Statistical Truths

If you wish to marry:

- ➤ You must insist on it.
- ➤ If you find yourself in a dead-end relationship, move on.
- ➤ Love yourself first.
- ➤ Commit yourself to the idea of getting married.
- ➤ Keep in shape, watch your weight, and take care of your appearance.
- ➤ Time can be your worst enemy. Use time wisely in your search for that marrying man.

Why Men Marry Some Women and Not Others

1

The Marrying Kind

WHEN BETH, one of my better researchers, said that men who were averse to commitment were drawn to her like bees to honey, I gave her a copy of the summary report of my research on "why men marry." The report showed that the primary reason a man asks one woman to marry and not another is that each woman treats him differently.

After looking it over for about fifteen minutes, Beth returned the report to my desk and told me I was a male chauvinist. I was taken aback for a moment. I was fond of Beth and trying to help her, so after I recovered, I asked her what made her think that.

She said, "You reinforce the myth that the reason men don't commit is that the women in their lives do something wrong. That's nonsense. In most cases, it's the man in a relationship who decides he isn't ready or doesn't want to get married, and he makes this decision without any help from the woman. No matter what some women do, there are certain men who are never going to commit. Unless you recognize that, you've missed the whole point. If you want to do women a real service, help us identify those losers before we get involved with them."

After telling Beth that more than three hundred women had worked with me on the marriage research and not one had made the comment she just offered, I apologized.

I had to admit she had a point. My interviews with single men had shown there *were* men who would not commit. Beth was also right when she said that if I could help women identify which men were more likely to commit, I would be performing a real service. As a reward for her insight, I put her in charge of the project.

Looking for Mr. Right

My researchers approached this project the same way we had others. First, Beth reviewed the literature and research we had on file. With this in mind, I reviewed our interviews with men and women who were planning to marry and videos of two focus groups we had run with single men. We then broadened the study by surveying and then running focus groups of single men who at that time had no intention of getting married. At first, we had young single men do the interviews, but so many of the interviewees gave macho answers that we doubted their reliability. In fact, we threw out the entire study and started again.

The second time we tried teams composed of men and women, but that produced mainly politically correct answers, which we also questioned. Finally, we had men in their sixties ask the questions, and that solved the problem. The responses they elicited were generally straightforward. The single men apparently did not feel an obligation to give these interviewers macho or politically correct answers.

Is He Old Enough to Marry?

This survey uncovered some interesting facts. The first was that there is an age when a man is ready to marry—the Age of Commitment. The age varies from man to man, but there are patterns that are easily identified:

> ➤ Most men who graduate from high school start thinking of marriage as a real possibility when they are twenty-three or twenty-four.

> ➤ Most men who graduate from college don't start considering marriage as a real possibility until age twenty-six.

> ➤ When men go to graduate school, it takes them longer to get into the working world, and they're not ready to get married until a few years after that.

> ➤ Ninety percent of men who have graduated from college are ready for the next step between ages twenty-six and thirty-three; this is when they are most likely to consider marriage. But this window of opportunity stays open only for four to five years, and then the chances a man will marry start to decline.

> ➤ A majority of college graduates between twenty-eight and thirty-three are in their high-commitment years and likely to propose.

> ➤ This period for well-educated men lasts just a bit over five years. The chances men will commit are sightly less when they are thirty-one or thirty-two than when they were between twenty-eight and thirty, but they're still in a high-commitment phase.

➤ Once men reach thirty-three or thirty-four, the chances they'll commit start to diminish, but only slightly. Until men reach thirty-seven, they remain very good prospects.

➤ After age thirty-eight, the chances they will ever marry drop dramatically.

➤ The chances that a man will marry for the first time diminish even more once he reaches forty-two or forty-three. At this point, many men become confirmed bachelors.

➤ Once men reach age forty-seven to fifty without marrying, the chances they will marry do not disappear, but they drop dramatically.

Still, there is no one-to-one correlation. For example, when a man goes to law school, which takes three additional years, he usually starts considering marriage around age twenty-seven or twenty-eight. That's also the age when most doctors, who spend four years in medical school and at least one year as an intern, start seriously thinking about marriage.

The single men we interviewed explained that when they get out of school and get a job and start making money, new possibilities open to them. For the first time, a majority of them have some independence. All of a sudden, they have a nice car and an apartment and an income. They're reluctant to even consider marriage for a few years, because they want to sow their wild oats. Many look at time spent as a carefree bachelor as a rite of passage. So for the first few years that they're on their own, their primary goal is having fun, which translates into dating without any serious thoughts about marriage.

Just Because You're Ready Doesn't Mean That He Is

One of the most common mistakes young women make is to assume that because they're ready for marriage in their early- or mid-twenties, the men they date are, as well. But as the above research shows, that's usually not the case. If a woman is seriously trying to find a husband, she should date men who have reached the age of commitment. She can date men slightly before they reach that age, because by the time she's gone out with a man for a year, he may have reached the point of being receptive to the idea of marriage. But this is taking a gamble that the man is typical, because the figures I've just given are educated estimates. Not all men mature at the same rate, and other factors can and do affect a man's readiness to marry. Even among men who are positively inclined toward marriage and are from identical educational and socioeconomic backgrounds, 20 percent will reach the age of commitment a year or more before our estimates, while another 20 percent will only consider marriage as a real option two to four years later. So if you're dating a man much younger than the commitment age, the chance he'll commit is relatively small.

There's one exception to this rule: Men and women who are seriously committed couples while still in school often get married shortly after they finish their formal education. This is usually an arrangement agreed to by the man but devised by the woman. Such couples, however, represent a very small percentage of today's singles.

Signing Off on the Scene

When we conducted a focus group with twelve men who had just proposed to women, we learned that men were far more likely to marry when they got tired of the singles scene. Our original intent was to determine how men at different ages reacted to single women they met at social gatherings. We started by asking the men about their lives before they met their future wives. How often and whom had they dated, where had they met the women, had they gone to singles places and, if so, how often? The first thing that struck us was that about a third of them said that for six months to two years before they met their brides-to-be, they were not dating or going to singles places as often as they had been just a few years earlier.

They had not stopped dating. It's just that they were no longer going to singles hangouts and trying to pick up women several times a week. Picking up women was no longer their main reason for going out. A majority of them hadn't admitted it to themselves, but their answers revealed they were trying to meet someone with whom they could have a serious relationship. They told us the singles scene was not as much fun as it used to be.

The Next Step

The men had not completely given up on the singles scene, but they were ready for "something else" or the "next step." Those two phrases caught my attention. Four of them used one phrase or the other, and ten of twelve men in our focus group said they felt the same way: The singles scene had lost some of its appeal. The "next step," as a majority of them admitted reluctantly to our researchers, was a serious relationship and possibly marriage.

We asked them why they weren't enjoying the singles scene, and at first the only answer we got was, "Been there, done that." Even though most of the men we met after they picked up a marriage license were between twenty-seven and thirty-four, we did meet men from seventeen to seventy-seven who were about to marry. Indeed, there was such a wide range of ages that at first we didn't think age was a factor. But it became clear that they weren't going to singles places as much as they had in the past because most of the people there were much younger than they were. Many men reluctantly admitted that for more than a year, they had felt uncomfortable in the singles world where they had been hanging out for the past five years. The singles world for professionals obviously is an older and more sophisticated crowd than that for men whose formal education ended in high school, but eventually men from both groups had the same experience.

Three young men who had graduated from the same high school were in one focus group made up of men who were about to marry. Two had taken some technical training; the third hadn't. One was a plumber, one worked repairing computers, and the third was a store manager. Each said he had begun to feel uncomfortable in his favorite singles place about two years earlier. For two of them, their singles place was a bar and pool hall where they and their single friends hung out and met women. The third man was a very active member of a large Baptist church. For him, the singles scene was church meetings and church singles functions. Interestingly, he and the fellows who frequented bars and pool halls made the same comment. One said that the singles bar he used to visit was filled with teenyboppers, and he felt out of place. He didn't say he had outgrown the bar; instead he complained that they weren't checking IDs anymore. The Baptist man observed that church dances were now attended by a bunch of "kids." All three admitted under questioning that when they had started hanging out in "their" singles place, they too were teenyboppers or kids. They had simply gotten too old for the crowd.

There were two single professionals in the same focus group, one a doctor and the other an engineer with a master's in electrical engineering and business administration. It surprised us when they reported feelings identical to those of the younger high-school-educated men. The places the professional single men went drew an older crowd. Among the professionals, the youngest women were college graduates and probably at least twenty-two. Professional men—unlike the younger men who had only completed high school—were perfectly at ease in their favorite singles places well into their thirties. Still, 30 percent of the single men with a postgraduate education said that as they approached thirty, they began to feel they no longer fit into their singles scene.

So there is a point at which men are likely to be ready for the next step, but the specific age depends on the man's maturity, education, and profession.

There were two notable exceptions to the age guidelines: men who were balding or heavy. Losing hair or putting on weight often makes men look older, and when a man looks older in singles places, he is often treated by the women as if he doesn't belong. Many men in their midtwenties who were getting bald said they weren't as interested in the singles scene as their buddies, and they were ready for a more serious relationship.

A twenty-four-year-old man who was almost completely bald explained that he had felt uncomfortable in the singles scene after he had approached a young woman in a singles bar and asked if he could buy her a drink. Her response was to tell him, loud enough for everyone in the bar to hear, that it would be a good idea if he went home and kissed his wife and played with his kids. When he protested, she became sarcastic. He could see he was losing the argument not only with her but with the entire bar. He walked out and never went back.

It is not how old they are that makes men uncomfortable, it is how old they feel, or how old others make them feel. Once a man decides he's too old for the singles scene, that part of his life is over, and he is more likely to marry.

Not Your Average Joe

Joe's experience was not unique. An attorney, he told us he had been going to a restaurant-bar for three years on Friday nights. It was a hangout for attorneys, judges, and others who worked in the court system. Joe explained that the restaurant was usually full, and on Friday nights the bar area was crowded with young singles, while most of those seated at tables were older and married. When he showed up one Friday night, there was a new hostess seating people. Without asking, she seated him at a table, assuming he wouldn't want to join the singles at the bar. Joe was too embarrassed to contradict her, and he realized she was right—he no longer belonged at the bar.

Most of the men we interviewed, however, asserted that they hadn't become convinced they were too old for the singles scene because of one incident. It was a series of small incidents over a period of time that turned them off—usually comments made by one or more young women that made them realize they no longer fit into the place they had frequented for years.

One of the focus groups composed of men about to marry said that if a woman wants to know whether a man is ready to get married, she should ask him how much he enjoys the singles scene. If he says it isn't as much fun as it used to be, he's a very good prospect, because he's ready to move on to the next step. They were right, but there's more to it than that: The woman should also ask the man a number of questions, including his age.

Bachelors for Life?

It's easy to spot a confirmed bachelor. He's so used to living alone that he will list the pleasures of the solo life—coming and going as he pleases, not answering to anyone—as reasons for not marrying. But there's still hope. Thousands of former "confirmed" bachelors get married each year, usually to women they've known for less than a year or whom they've been going with for many years. Once men reach age forty-seven to fifty without marrying, the chances they will marry do not disappear, but they drop dramatically.

Please keep in mind that I'm talking about men who have never been married. Men who have been married before are open to remarry much later in life. They have entirely different relationships with women. (You'll find more on them in chapter 7.)

If a woman in her forties or older who has never been married is dating a man who has never been married, the chance of him marrying is still good. But at that time in her life, most eligible men are either widowed or divorced, and their chances of marrying again are substantially higher than those of men of the same age who have never married. In other words, if a woman meets two men in their late forties, one who has been married and the other a lifelong bachelor, she should choose the one who has been married before. Although the first man may on the surface appear more cautious, he's far more likely to marry than the second. Many single women say divorced men are often bitter and defensive, so they don't date them. That's usually a mistake.

Handling Stringers

If you're dating a man who has had one or more long-term relationships with other women and didn't marry them, there's a real possibility he's a stringer. A stringer is a man who strings women along. He likes having a woman, sleeping with a woman, eating with a woman, possibly sharing his life with a woman without ever making a real commitment. He often tells women, up front, he never intends to marry, so if and when he decides he wants to cut out, she has no reason to complain.

If you think you may be involved with a stringer, establish a deadline. If he doesn't commit to you within six months, get rid of him. Pay no attention to his excuses. He may tell you that you're coming on too strong. He may complain that the two of you haven't been going together long enough, that he doesn't know, that he hasn't made up his mind. In fact, he is likely to tell you anything that will get you to stick around without his needing to make a commitment. Don't fall for it. The chances a stringer will marry are very slim; he is simply not the marrying kind.

Earlier I mentioned those men who went with one woman for a time, then shortly thereafter went out and married another. This was the pattern, in fact, that initiated our research. So we questioned the couples in which the man had gone with one woman for years and was marrying another. The women who married these men insisted they commit early in the relationship.

If you meet a man who has had a long-term relationship, make it clear to him that if he dates you for a certain length of time, you'll expect a ring. If he doesn't understand that, you haven't done your job. Don't think his affirmative response to such a declaration is a precursor to his making a commitment. He's strung many women along, and he may try it with you. If after six months you don't have a firm commitment, leave.

We ran across at least fifty men we could identify as stringers. They can be very dangerous. I estimate each one is responsible for at least two women remaining single. They are destructive because they con women into wasting their time during the years when they are most attractive and most likely to get a proposal. They stay with women, live with women, promise them marriage, and string them on and on indefinitely.

There is one surefire way to identify these men—they are usually repeat offenders. If a man had even one long-term relationship with someone else, he's very likely to be a stringer. If he does not set a firm date, be on your guard.

Biological Clocks

We spoke to 121 men in their forties who were marrying for the first time. Their reason for marrying was different than that of the younger men we interviewed. Many of these older men were eager to marry because their biological clock was running. Obviously, a man's biological clock isn't the same as a woman's, but men are often in just as much of a hurry to have children. They're not worried about physically being able to father a child, but about *being* a father to the child. Men forty-two and older who were about to marry looked forward to having children, and they almost unanimously pictured themselves as fathers of sons. They want to be young enough when their sons come along to teach them all the things fathers traditionally teach their sons—to ride a bicycle, to fish, to play ball, and so forth. The most important reason these men had for marrying was that if they waited much longer, they wouldn't be able to be active fathers. So if you meet a man in his forties who tells you he's eager to have a son so he can do those male-bonding things, know that these things are very important to him, and they'll dramatically increase his readiness to marry.

Unpolished Jewels

We talked to dozens of men in their late thirties and early forties who had given up on the idea of marrying. Most lacked one of three things—looks, height, or social skills. They had been rejected so often that they had despaired of ever finding a woman who would love them or even put up with them. Many had been treated cruelly by women. If I heard it once, I heard it a dozen times: "If I could find a nice woman, I'd marry her tomorrow." If you meet a man who has never been married and seems excessively shy, it doesn't mean he's not interested in you, particularly if he's in his late thirties or older and not socially gifted. If you signal your own interest, you may find a nice guy who would love to settle down.

These men have been rejected and demeaned for years by women because they weren't tall enough or handsome enough or smooth enough. It's easy to understand why they're so reluctant to put their egos on the line once more. If you meet a man who appeals to you, don't let his lack of social skills dissuade you from showing you're interested in him. Only after being convinced you like him will he be able to summon the courage to ask you for a date. You may even end up having to do the asking, but it might be worthwhile: These "diamonds in the rough" are often strong candidates for marriage.

There are literally hundreds of thousands of men and women in their forties and fifties eagerly seeking mates, but somehow they can't seem to find each other. The main reason, I believe, is that those in both groups have been emotionally battered in the dating game, and they're very gun-shy. If you can help a man overcome these feelings, you may find a real diamond in the rough. I know it's a hard thing for a woman to do, but if you can put yourself on the line just once more, you might be rewarded with a wonderful guy.

One thing impressed me: The men who were not married were just as nice, just as intelligent, just as hardworking as the men who were. Maybe that's why seven out of eight men aged fifty and over who were about to marry for the first time were marrying women who had been divorced. These women told us they saw lack of social skills or a few inches in height as a minor detail, because they had already had a man who was tall or suave, and he hadn't made a very good husband.

Bad Investments

There is a possible drawback to dating a man aged forty or older. Many men at that age begin to look at women and marriage as a poor financial investment. There's no other way of putting it. When you ask them why they're not married, they tell you they spent most of their lives building a nest egg, and they're not about to share it with some "babe." In our interviews, they often used such derogatory terms when speaking of women. They talked as though a woman's only interest in a man is what she can get out of him. The irony is that many of the men who spoke this way really didn't have all that much anyway. Today, many of the women whom these men think are after their money earn far more than they do. If a man talks of marriage as a financial game in which women are out to make their fortunes, don't just walk away—run! Such men are hardly ever going to be the marrying kind.

I'm not suggesting money is a subject that couples shouldn't discuss when they're thinking about marriage. All couples need to discuss money, especially when either partner has assets and responsibilities. Just don't base the discussion on the assumption that either one is out to take advantage of the other.

Parents' Marriage

Another factor that determines whether a man is likely to get married is the success, or lack thereof, of his parents' marriage. This, of course, affects women as well. We found that many single men and women in their late thirties and forties were products of divorce. With the men, in most cases their parents' marriage broke up when they were young, and it seemed to have affected the way they looked at life. The difference between older children of divorce and other confirmed bachelors is their reason for not being married. Older single men whose parents had a good marriage say, "I'm not getting married because I'm not ready," "I'm not the marrying type," "I enjoy being single."

Older unmarried men who are products of divorce complain about marriage itself. They'd like to get married, they say, but they don't have much faith in the institution; it's not all it's cracked up to be. They believe in living together, because in their minds, once people marry, the romance ends. They usually don't keep their feelings a secret. If you talk with them about marriage, they tend to be very open about what they believe. Men from divorced homes do marry, but they're a bit reluctant to do so. Often the women had to drag them to the altar. Obviously, since it plays such an important role in a man's decision making, the marital status of a man's parents is one of the first things you want to find out.

(If you'd like to investigate further the effect of divorce on adult children, read *The Unexpected Legacy of Divorce* by Judith Wallerstein, a book I discovered after I had completed my research.)

None of this is to suggest that if you meet a man whose parents were divorced, you should immediately cross him off your list. About half the people in America fall into that category, and you'd end up with a very short list. But it's definitely one of the things you should bear in mind and ask about when you are dating a man you're considering marrying. I can't tell you exactly how much impact it will have on any particular man's decision to marry, but I know it can be a big stumbling block.

Socioeconomic Factors

Another crucial factor that influences the chances of a couple marrying is socioeconomic mix. If both members of a dating couple come from the same or a similar background, they're substantially more likely to get married than if their backgrounds are dissimilar. Date men who will fit in with your friends and business associates. Opposites may *attract,* but men and women from similar backgrounds *marry.*

So bear in mind that a man is much more likely to marry you if he is from the same socioeconomic background as you are.

When Religion and Politics Mix

Other factors that contribute to the likelihood of a relationship leading to marriage are religious beliefs and political persuasion. Each of these has a relative value. If a man is deeply committed to his religion, he probably won't marry outside that religion unless the woman gives in to him on religious matters. The same goes for a woman with strong ties to a religion; her fiancé may need to accept her faith. In some cases, this means one person converting to the other's religion. The most common impediment to marriage is one party's insistence that the children be raised in his or her faith. So if you're dating someone from another religion and both of you hold your religious beliefs very strongly, it dramatically reduces the chance that you will marry.

Couples coming out of marriage license bureaus confirmed these findings. A number of them told us that before they met their intended, they had had a serious relationship in which religious differences caused one party to break it off. I'm not suggesting there aren't interreligious marriages; I have friends and family whose interreligious marriages work very well. But it's a statistical fact that commonly held religious beliefs increase the likelihood a couple will marry.

Therefore, if you have a choice of dating two men who seem equally desirable, but one holds the same religious beliefs you do and the other doesn't, you're better off dating the man with beliefs similar to yours. Your chances of marrying him are much greater than your chances of marrying the other man.

The importance of belief systems cannot be underestimated,

and this is also demonstrated in political areas. Men and women often do not cross "party lines" on the way to the altar: Republicans generally marry Republicans, Democrats marry Democrats, conservatives marry conservatives, and liberals marry liberals. Of course, there are exceptions. One of the most public party-crossing couples is conservative pundit Mary Matalin and Democratic campaign manager James Carville, who worked for opposite sides when Democrat Bill Clinton challenged GOP incumbent George H. W. Bush for the presidency.

In the focus group we put together to investigate political alignments in marriage, we discovered that many married couples were politically divided. We know more women vote Democratic than men, and more men vote Republican than women. Political disagreements are a significant factor only when they're grounded in core beliefs. Differences of opinions on core values such as abortion, capital punishment, or even disciplining children can divide a couple.

So if your deeply held values and beliefs, religious or political, clash with those of your man, it's less likely that you will wed. Think it over. People with similar beliefs and values tend to have similar outlooks on life and are usually more compatible.

Living at Home

Men who live at home with their parents are less likely to marry than men who have their own places. This is more significant in some communities than in others. In communities where circumstances make it difficult for young people to find a suitable place to live—for example, an expensive suburb where there are no rentals—it isn't as important. Nevertheless, a man who lives alone is more likely to marry than one who lives with his parents. We also discovered that men who have never lived away from home are less likely to marry than men who have. Men who have gone away to college or have worked in a different city are more likely to marry than men who have never left their parents' home.

Following the Pack

Another important question a woman should ask a man before getting serious is whether any of his male friends have married in the last year or so. If so, there's a substantially higher chance that he himself will tie the knot within the next two years than if none of his buddies has recently renounced bachelorhood. More than 60 percent of the men we questioned coming out of marriage license bureaus told us they had a friend who had married within the last year.

After we asked men in singles bars if any of their friends had recently married, and if they themselves were considering getting married, we saw a reason for this correlation. Seeing their friends marrying had clearly caused a change in their thinking. Those who said none of their male friends was married were two to three times as likely to tell our researchers they were not ready to marry. Of those who had seen even a few male friends get married recently, a majority said if they met the right woman, they might think seriously about getting married. There's no question men play follow-the-leader when it comes to marriage.

Keeping It in the Family

A follow-the-leader factor can also be seen in families. Single men who had unmarried older siblings—particularly if the siblings were still living at home and past the prime marrying age—were less likely to find a spouse than men whose older siblings were married, or those men who had no older siblings.

Men usually will tell you what they think. If a man says he does not see himself married, could never see himself married, doesn't think marriage is for him, you should look elsewhere.

Date Only the Marrying Kind

To dramatically increase your chances of marrying you must seek out and date the marrying kind.

Statistical Truths About the Marrying Kind

> ➤ Most men will not even consider marriage before they reach the age of commitment. For 80 percent of high school graduates, the minimum age of commitment is twenty-three, whereas for 80 percent of college graduates, it's twenty-six.

> ➤ The high-commitment period for most college-educated men is from ages twenty-eight to thirty-three.

> ➤ For men who go to graduate school—doctors, lawyers, and the like—the high-commitment period runs from thirty to thirty-six.

> ➤ After age thirty-seven or thirty-eight, the chance that a man will commit diminishes. After forty-three, it diminishes even more.

> ➤ Most men think sowing their wild oats is a rite of passage and will not even contemplate marriage until they

have been working and living as independent adults for several years.

➤ Men are most likely to marry after they become uncomfortable with the singles scene.

➤ Men have biological clocks. They want to be young enough to teach their sons to fish and play ball, and to do the male-bonding thing.

➤ Men who look at marriage as a financial arrangement in which women have the most to gain are not likely to marry—nor are they good prospects. Run . . . fast.

➤ Men whose parents divorced when they were young are often gun-shy about marrying.

➤ Men often marry women whose backgrounds— religion, politics, values, socioeconomic status— match theirs.

➤ Men who have their own places and have lived as independent, self-supporting adults are more likely to marry.

➤ Men whose friends and siblings are married are more likely to marry.

➤ If a man over the age of forty has been married before, he is more likely to marry than a forty-year-old man who has never been married.

➤ If you wish to facilitate a trip to the altar, meet and date only the marrying kind!

2

First Impressions

EVERY SPEAKER wants to draw as large an audience as possible, and I'm no exception. I love it when the room is filled with people. Still, a few years back when I approached a room in which I was scheduled to speak, I was surprised by the overflow crowd—there were at least as many people in the hallway as there were in the room.

I started by asking the audience why they were there. A very attractive young woman in the first row asked if I remembered Margie from the Chicago office inquiring whether the popularity sales skills I was teaching would work in a social setting. I explained that I speak to more than a hundred audiences a year, so I didn't remember Margie. Then she asked: Would practicing looking positive, upbeat, and pleasant make a woman more attractive to men? I said I was almost sure it would. She said, "That's what you told Margie, and that's why we're here."

I found out later that after I had given Margie that advice, she and half a dozen other single women in her company had decided to test my theory. They agreed to meet every Friday at lunch in one of the conference rooms to practice looking pleasant, friendly, and positive. After the first meeting, they decided it would be helpful to practice at home for a week before meeting again. The following Friday, each of them would role-play meeting three different men for the first time. The women critiqued one another's performances and made suggestions for improvement.

They ran these meetings once a week for six weeks before they had to stop. Word had leaked out of what they were doing, and dozens of women began showing up—far too many for such an intimate format to work well.

These meetings were based on a handout I used when training salespeople. I had knocked off the handout in a few hours when a salesperson told me he had forgotten exactly what he should practice at home after going to one of my training sessions.

The little handout proved very helpful. Some salespeople used it to practice, whereas others read it over before a major presentation. Most agreed it taught them how to make a good first impression.

The importance of making a positive first impression on anyone—potential client or potential mate—cannot be emphasized enough. When we asked men who had just gotten engaged what attracted them to their fiancées when they first met, most said it was how classy, positive, energetic, enthusiastic, and upbeat their future wives were. Over and over, we heard answers such as, "She was so vivacious," or "She was enthusiastic"—or "bubbly," or "friendly." "I was immediately attracted to her," many of them told us. Interestingly, while 68 percent gave some sort of physical description of the woman they were about to marry, only about 20 percent of those men described their future wives as gorgeous or sexy, whereas more than 60 percent described their personalities. That was what attracted most of them in the first place. Even men who were marrying very beautiful women were more likely to emphasize their fiancée's personality over her physical beauty. They typically said things such as:

- ➤ "I took one look at her, and I knew she was the kind of person I wanted to be with."
- ➤ "She was so well mannered."
- ➤ "She was the kind of person any guy would be proud to be with."
- ➤ "She was enthusiastic."
- ➤ "She was so full of the joy of life."
- ➤ "She seemed so at ease with the world."
- ➤ "She was the kind of woman you could take anywhere and be proud."
- ➤ "When she talked, I felt so good."
- ➤ "I didn't know if we'd become lovers, but I was sure we'd be friends."
- ➤ "It was a joy being around her."
- ➤ "She was poised" (or *energetic, decent, kind, articulate, clever, entertaining . . .*).

I don't mean to understate the effect of physical beauty; there is no question it attracts men. But even when they first meet a woman, it's usually the woman's personality that makes her seem special. The words men used most often to describe their fiancées were *classy, nice, friendly, kind, elegant, self-assured, poised,* and so forth. As it happens, in most cases the men using these words were not themselves poised, elegant, self-assured, or classy. Nor were their fiancées, in reality. But that was the way the men perceived the women they planned to marry when they first met. It's critical that your first impression on a man be a positive one, because it often determines how he will see you from that moment on.

Marrying Up

Whether they've grown up in poor, crime-ridden neighborhoods or upscale suburbs, men want to marry women who are in some ways their better. A majority of men want the woman they marry to meet their ideas of refinement, elegance, and decency. Often those are the reasons they were attracted to her in the first place.

Men brag about the women they are about to marry; for many, their future spouse is a status symbol. The whole idea that only gorgeous young women are trophy wives is nonsense. All wives are "trophy wives." When we interviewed grooms-to-be, to the astonishment of my mainly female research team members, the main message the men conveyed was that they were proud of their brides.

A great example of this was two particular grooms who at first glance seemed to have nothing in common. A researcher and I met them outside a marriage license bureau in Florida. One was the son of a former congressman. He was also third-generation old money, a graduate of an Ivy League law school. The second was raised by a single mother in the inner city.

The bride of the second man could not stop telling us how he had transformed himself from a gang member to a man with a steady job. The researcher who interviewed her said she beamed when she announced he had just been promoted in the Fortune 500 company he worked for. She started by telling the researchers he had quit school in the ninth grade and had to work very hard to earn his GED. When I interviewed him, he bragged that he had passed the test for the post office on his first try. But, he added, if he had not, he would have kept on taking it until he did. He then went to community college at night, and after completing his course applied for his present job.

The first man told us he worked with very rich and powerful people, so the woman he married had to be very special. Then he explained with obvious pride that his bride would fit into his world because she was as accomplished as any woman he had ever encountered. He boasted about how wonderful she was with people. He told us of how she had shown grace and poise when she helped him entertain two dozen of his clients. He found it difficult to believe she was only twenty-five. This rather sophisticated man—a true blueblood—said it was his experience that women from the best families and the best schools usually don't achieve that degree of sophistication until well into their thirties. He informed us that she had handled some of the richest and most powerful people in the world with the grace and artistry of a grande dame.

Immediately, the man raised in a slum chimed in, "I know just what you mean. I was blown away by my girl's sophistication, too. We went to a restaurant, and she put her napkin in her lap and ordered me to put mine on my lap. Wow—she almost knocked me off my #@*&# chair."

I use these two men as examples for several reasons. Both women were very attractive, but neither man mentioned it. These very different men made statements that reflected the feelings of 46 percent of the men we interviewed coming out of marriage license bureaus. This convinced the female researchers that men are not quite as shallow as most women believe.

But the main reason I cite these men is that both—along with almost half of the others who had just gotten engaged—said they knew there was something special about their women as soon as they met. Like nearly half the men we interviewed, these men admitted that sexual attraction was a factor in their choice of a bride, but claimed it was not what clinched their decision.

Making a Good First Impression

When you walk into a room, have a pleasant look on your face, but not a big grin. Why not? If you have a big smile on your face when you walk in but the minute you start talking to someone that smile disappears, it sends the message that you don't like the person you are speaking with. Smiling is important, but most people, especially women, need to tone it down. What generally works best is the look you get on your face when you're *about* to smile. Then you can break into a real grin when you meet someone, which lets him know you really are pleased to meet him.

One of the keys to making a good first impression is to match your verbal with your nonverbal messages. When you say, "Pleased to meet you," you need to look and sound pleased. A majority of those we surveyed told us they were attracted to people who seemed to like them. It sounds very simple, but it's a little trickier than it sounds.

About 80 percent of the people we surveyed thought they could charm others if they set out to do so. But research shows that when most people deliberately turn on the charm, they smile too broadly, and the people they meet see their smiles as artificial. Rather than create a positive impression, they either create no impression at all or, worse, turn off the very people they intended to charm. We found that many women come across as overly friendly, something you should be careful to avoid.

Practice being charming in front of a full-length mirror. Start by trying to look like a person everybody likes. It may take a while, possibly several sessions of ten to fifteen minutes, but almost everyone who role-plays being upbeat and friendly in front of a mirror eventually ups her charm quotient considerably.

Second Impressions

What I refer to as a "second impression," most people would call the second part of the first impression—and they're right. The division is artificial, but it lets us break down a first impression into teachable elements.

The first element of a first impression is primarily nonverbal. It's the message you send when you walk into a room, before you open your mouth. Obviously, first impressions are not always nonverbal. Often when you meet someone for the first time, you shake hands and start to speak immediately. But it's easier to learn the nonverbal elements of a first impression separately from the verbal parts. That's how the young women who practiced the nonverbal elements outlined in my sales training manual made themselves more attractive to men. The women had mastered sending signals that created a good first impression. In fact, they learned to turn on those signals at will, which enabled them to charm not only men but just about anyone they met, as well. As you might imagine, they found it a very useful talent.

Several skills you can master with relative ease will help you create a good second impression: a good handshake, a friendly recognition glance, smooth, measured movements, a pleasing voice, conversation skills, listening skills, and the ability to send a friendly message. I could spend a chapter on these skills, but a few simple instructions will suffice.

If you're not sure of your handshake, practice it with both male and female friends. When you first catch a person's eye, an *I-am-about-to-smile* look announces that you're friendly. While you don't want your movements to be quick or jerky so you appear nervous or unsure, you don't want to appear stiff or dull either. Try making a video of yourself greeting people, and become your own body-language coach.

Next, record yourself speaking in different situations. Go to a speech teacher if you don't like what you hear. (Make sure you find someone qualified. Go to a local college or university and hire someone from the speech department as a coach.) If you aren't a good conversationalist, become an expert on one or two noncontroversial topics that interest most people, such as sports, the arts, the latest best-selling book or hit movie, the stock market—any subject you believe will interest people. (Avoid religion and politics until you become more comfortable.) Then say a few words about the topics. Be confident without being pompous. Keep your remarks short and leave "air space" for the other person to respond. Good conversationalists are good listeners, and good listeners spend at least three times as much time listening as they do speaking.

Role-play the part of a pleasant, friendly person while speaking into the tape recorder for ten to fifteen minutes every day for two to three weeks. It's important that you don't just look friendly and upbeat but sound friendly and upbeat, as well. Try not to judge your voice. You're used to hearing yourself in your own head, and most of us sound better there than anywhere else. Many people are unpleasantly surprised by what they hear, while others miss obvious flaws such as an unflattering accent.

Ask friends for their opinion or—even better if you can arrange it—get more objective feedback from strangers. Give your tape to a friend and ask him or her to play it for someone who doesn't know you, then solicit from the listener their impression of the person on the tape. If the description is negative, work on improving and retest. The good news is, almost everyone improves—some dramatically—within a few months. If you don't see improvement, take acting classes, or put yourself in situations where you're meeting strangers on a casual basis in low-risk settings that almost force you to interact—volunteer to help organize a local charity event, for example.

Unfortunately, to create a good second impression, you'll need to master at least one very difficult skill: You have to maintain that pleasant, friendly look. It is harder than it sounds. Once you stop thinking about looking friendly, you're likely to fall into old habits, coming across as your old, less approachable self. The message most of us send is no message at all: *I'm not happy or unhappy, I'm simply here.* Worse, 20 percent of us, without realizing it, send the message that we're *un*happy and do not care for most of the people we meet. The main reason men don't like women when they first meet is that the women nonverbally announce they do not like the men. That isn't the message most women want to send or think they're sending, but it's all too common.

Old habits are hard to break, and how you hold your facial muscles is just another habit. After you've mastered looking friendly and upbeat in front of a mirror, practice doing so two to three times a week for fifteen minutes. Once you can maintain a pleasant expression on your face for an extended period in front of a mirror, you can move to the next exercise.

Role-play meeting men in front of a mirror. The goal of this exercise is making that pleasant and positive expression part of your everyday life. You want that look to become your everyday "walk-around" face—the face you wear when you go to the supermarket, mop the floor, shine your shoes, eat lunch, talk to a friend, attend business functions, and, of course, encounter men you would like to meet. It should become as natural as breathing. You will have succeeded when you can maintain that pleasant expression without thinking about it—unless, of course, you have good reason for not looking pleasant.

After the mirror work, the best way to make that positive look a permanent part of you is to record yourself with a video camera, trying to maintain that upbeat, friendly look and sound. After fifteen or twenty minutes, play back the video and see how well you've done. Don't despair—most people have to practice in front of a mirror repeatedly, using a video camera to test their progress. It's far more difficult to maintain your new pleasant expression on camera and in real life than in front of a mirror.

Just as with other forms of exercise, you need to build endurance. Once you're able to maintain your new face for a minute, practice two minutes in front of the mirror and then two minutes on videotape. Keep doing this until you can maintain your friendly expression in front of a camera easily for ten minutes.

The mirror helps monitor your nonverbal messages, and this improves your performance. Don't become discouraged by your first sight of yourself on camera. More than 90 percent of those I have known who practice using a video camera make life-changing improvements.

If in addition to looking and sounding positive and friendly, you hold yourself erect without becoming stiff when sitting, standing, and walking, people will find you more attractive. This usually is not too difficult for women, who generally have better posture than men. Still, we found it was necessary for members of both sexes, if they wanted to create a great first impression, to monitor their posture. Start by videotaping yourself while you're sitting, standing, and walking. If possible, have a friend or family member videotape you when you're not aware you're on camera.

It's not a matter of remaining West Point ramrod straight. That doesn't send a positive message; it says, *I am stiff and uptight.* Keep your head erect and your shoulders back. The best way for a woman to do this is to put a book on her head and a tightly rolled washcloth on each shoulder. Practice moving from place to place while keeping all three balanced. When you can keep both the book and the washcloths in place for ten minutes—or better still, when you can keep them in place without even thinking about it—go to the next step. Sit with them in place. Wear them while you watch television or do some desk work until you can keep them in place without effort.

Erect posture says to most people that you're positive and self-assured, which in turn makes you more attractive. Men like women who like themselves.

When you've mastered these skills, you'll have no trouble making a good first and second impression. Life in general will become easier.

Charm Crosses Over

Sending positive nonverbal and verbal signals not only makes you more attractive to men but also helps you marry. I knew the exercises in my sales training brochure had done this for some women, and I assumed it would work for others as well. I was right—and the results were better than I would have guessed. Since the afternoon Margie asked me about using sales skills in social settings, at least three hundred women who tried it reported back that it had worked.

Once you learn to make a good first impression in a business setting, the skill is transferable to social situations.

What Your Clothes Say

Of course, what you choose to wear is just as important as the body-language messages you send. I tested the class message sent by women's clothing and its impact on the people they meet years ago while researching the *Dress for Success* books. I assumed the reaction that took place in a business setting would be similar to the one that occurred in a social setting, and I was right. As we've seen, men are much more likely to approach a woman if she is dressed in an outfit with which he is comfortable. Men are more likely to marry women from a background similar to theirs—but it's usually women they perceive as their "betters" in social situations.

A perfect example is seen in the movie *Working Girl.* Melanie Griffith plays a twenty-something secretary from a blue-collar family who meets and charms a successful businessman—played by Harrison Ford—from an upper-middle class background. When we first meet her, she is wearing cheap clothing and jewelry, overdone "big" hair, and inappropriate makeup. They all scream *blue collar.* Then she undergoes a makeover. She starts dressing in expensive-looking, understated clothing similar to what her older female boss wears; she loses the processed hairdo for a short, neat executive style; and finally she tones down her makeup. In real life, she would have had to spend more time working on her body language and verbal patterns, but nevertheless the effect is spectacular. It makes the relationship between the two characters, who are obviously going to be lovers, believable.

We all judge people by the way they present themselves. When a man meets a woman for the first time, he reacts in a predictable way to her body language, facial expression, speech patterns, and clothing. He has been conditioned by the other women he has met, by Hollywood images, and by his background to make judgments based on how she looks. Sometimes those judgments are based on how he processes information, but just as often they are unconscious. No matter how he makes the judgments, they control his actions.

While sending an appropriate class message increases the chances that a first meeting will lead to a relationship, signaling that you are—to borrow a phrase from the older generation—a "proper young lady" is even more important. The men we talked to often described their fiancées as "decent," "family-oriented," or what I refer to as "situational virgins." More than 80 percent of the men we put in focus groups who were getting married in 1999 sooner or later said or even bragged that the women they were going to marry were the kind of woman you would be proud to introduce to friends and family. There was no question they were talking about the women's virtue. You could tell by the vocabulary the men used when describing women they would *not* marry—women who by their standards were "loose," "easy," or worse. Those who were more broad-minded replaced sexual virtue with social virtue. They described their fiancées as women they could take home to Mother or introduce to their bosses.

The Perils of Dressing for Sex

After they gave these descriptions, we asked men when they first realized that their fiancées were "nice girls." More than 70 percent told us they knew the minute they met, and almost half said or implied that this was what had first attracted them. The biggest surprise was that when asked to describe their fiancées when they first met them, 19 percent of the men described what the women were wearing. I've been research-ing clothing for more than thirty-five years, and never did more than 7 percent of the men questioned remember what anyone wore at a business meeting that had taken place more than three months earlier. More importantly, many of the men described their fiancées' outfits when explaining how they knew the women were virtuous. They made comments such as this:

> ➤ "She looked so determined to cure people in her crisp white [nurse's] uniform, I knew she was the type of girl I couldn't mess with."

> "Her suit made her look like a little girl dressed in Daddy's clothing, very proper but sexy as hell."

> "She was wearing jeans and a blouse with lace at the neck and cuffs. It made her look like an innocent little girl."

> "Her outfit wasn't revealing. In fact, it covered her from head to foot—but it was sexy."

> "I couldn't take my eyes off her. She was wearing this pink dress."

> "If you were picking a costume for an angel, that dress would be perfect."

The vast majority described clothing that announced the woman was respectable. Only seven men of the more than two thousand we questioned said their fiancée was dressed in a very sexy outfit when they met. This was backed up by the women, most of whom remembered what they were wearing when they first met their fiancés. Only a handful told us they were wearing a sexy outfit; most said what they were wearing was anything but sexy.

So if you are going to a social setting where you are likely to meet eligible men, choose a look that is not only attractive but also appropriate.

Dressing to Be a Wife, Not a One-Night Stand

As I explained earlier, when we finish with a self-contained element of research, we run our findings by the researchers to get their feedback. Most of our researchers were women, and they were convinced that while men claimed to be attracted to women who were not sending strong sexual signals, their collective experience had taught them the opposite was true. We then ran a focus group of women who were about to be married, and they more or less agreed with our female researchers.

We had to conduct two focus groups with men who were about to be married to convince these women that men *are* interested in the personal traits of women when they first meet. Our researchers did not want to believe the results from the first group, so we convened a second. The men in both groups agreed with the women that a sexy outfit will attract hordes of men, but they went on to explain—using crude language and bawdy humor—that they saw a sexy outfit as an invitation to have sex. What is more, a woman who dressed sexy but did not deliver was a tease, and they did not want to be involved with her.

A majority of the men who were about to marry put a woman on first meeting into one of two categories: those they bedded and those they wedded—this despite the fact that an overwhelming majority of their fiancées were not virgins when they met. While two women researchers held out for the politically correct point of view, most admitted that the double standard was alive and well in the (small) minds of most men.

What make this information so useful is that men usually make life-changing decisions that critically affect the nature of their relationships within ten minutes of meeting a woman. They decide whether this is the kind of woman with whom they might have a serious relationship before they really know her. Nearly half the men who had asked women to marry them told us they knew their bride-to-be was special as soon as they met her. Of the 50 percent remaining, almost half said they knew there was a possibility that the relationship could become serious before the second date. Of the remaining 27 percent, almost one-third could not remember at what point they had decided the woman they were about to marry was special. Yet even 73 percent of this group admitted that the first impression she made probably did sway their thinking. Even those who believed it took them a long time to make up their minds whether this was the woman for them admitted that their fiancée had not changed much since they first met. What this all means is that first impressions are both critical and long lasting.

Looking Past Looks

The other fact that our female researchers found hard to understand was that very attractive and successful men often married women who were neither attractive nor successful. When we first started measuring this phenomenon, we thought that men and women marrying each other were likely to be equally attractive. We also noted, however, that very attractive men and women often married people who were not attractive. The very attractive people we asked about this explained that all their lives, people a lot smarter and more talented than them had catered to them simply because of their looks, and they thought it was stupid. Women were more likely than men to see their looks as a gift of nature equal and in some ways superior to brains or talent. Most men had a different view. Sixty-seven percent of the very good-looking men we interviewed thought of their looks as a minor asset and told the researchers they would rather be smart, rich, or talented than good-looking.

If you want to marry a man who is more attractive than you, obeying four rules will increase your chances of success.

➤ First, *you* must approach *him*. Very attractive men seldom make passes at women—they don't have to. If they
just stand or sit by themselves, women will gather
around.

➤ Second, the very good-looking man, like other men,
enjoys doting on his woman. When you first meet him,
treat him as you would any other man, no better and
no worse.

➤ Third, without being boastful, make sure he knows
about your talents and accomplishments. Very good-
looking men often marry women who have qualities
they lack—education, professional accomplishment,
social standing, or ambition.

➤ Fourth, make demands on him. Insist that he go back
to school or try for a better job, for example. Give him a
bit of a push.

This discussion of good-looking men is part of a chapter on
first impressions because one in four very good-looking men
said that the women they were marrying let them know early
in the relationship that their good looks were not enough, and
that made those women special in their minds. The men were
impressed most with a woman who was friendly and self-
assured, but they saw her as special when she appeared com-
petent and able.

Meeting His Family

It is not enough to make a good impression on the man you
are dating; almost as important is making a good impression
on his family. I interviewed sixty-two men who said they

started thinking about marrying their fiancée only when their own relatives said she was something special. Justin recounted that after introducing his sisters to Jennifer one weekend, he showed up with another woman the next. The two sisters took their brother into another room, sat him down, and chastised him for letting Jennifer get away. After having met Jennifer briefly, the sisters had decided she was smarter and better educated and had more class than all the flighty women Justin had dated put together. Once he thought about it, Justin agreed and started dating Jennifer exclusively, he told us.

Justin's story was not unusual. Five percent of the men on their way to the altar told us that their family had convinced them that the woman they were going to marry was special. More than 30 percent said their family's positive opinion of the woman influenced them. In most cases, the family members knew the women for only a short time before making their judgments. Since you already know how to make a terrific first impression, that is the good news.

The bad news is that 11 percent of the newly engaged women told us they had had a previous relationship that they believed would have led to marriage had it not been for the groom's family. Almost half of these women were at least able to guess why the man's family objected to the relationship. Among the reasons they gave were religion, background, education, ethnicity, race, money, class, and the classic "No one is good enough for my boy." Whether the women thought the reasons were sound or a product of ignorance or prejudice makes no difference. They were convinced they did not usually turn people off when they met them, and if they were rejected for these reasons, the family's beliefs were out of their control. The remaining 56 percent, however, had no idea why the man's family disapproved of them after meeting them for just a few minutes or, at most, a few hours.

Obviously, they had not made a good first impression. After you have practiced the exercises outlined earlier, you should have few problems if you keep some rules in mind.

No matter where the first meeting with your man's family takes place, dress as if you're going to church and want to impress the minister. Be polite. Be correct. If you're not sure how to handle an introduction—who is to be introduced to whom—or which fork to use, read a book on etiquette beforehand. Greet the important people early. If you attend a gathering of his family, such as a wedding, make it a point to have him introduce you to his immediate family as soon as possible. Insist that he introduce you to everyone and stay with you for the first five minutes of any conversation. Do more listening than talking. Tell the man that unless you are getting along famously and want to stay, he is to break you away from any one person or group after no more than fifteen minutes. Limit yourself to one or two drinks no matter how much anyone else is drinking. Arrive on time and leave early.

Good luck. If you've done your part, the rest is out of your hands!

A Statistical Edge to Making a Good First Impression

➤ A restrained smile is better than a broad grin when you're trying to create a good first impression.

➤ The essentials to making a good first impression are a friendly facial expression, a good handshake, erect stature with smooth, easy movements, and a pleasant voice—and when you say you're pleased to meet someone, look as if you really are.

➤ Good posture says you are positive and self-assured. If you can maintain good posture while looking relaxed—not stiff or dull—men will find you more attractive and likable.

➤ Most of the women I coached, when they initially tried to make a good first impression, failed. But it took only a few hours of practice for them to get the hang of it.

➤ Maintaining the statistical edge of a good first impression involves sending friendly, positive verbal and nonverbal messages.

➤ The first impression made by a woman when she meets a man often determines the nature of the relationship that follows.

➤ The main reason men are turned off by women when they first meet is the women, usually without realizing it, announce nonverbally that they do not like the men. Men most often like women who like them.

➤ Men are attracted by the physical but marry character.

➤ All wives are trophy wives. Strive to be someone a man admires and likes to show off.

➤ Dressing appropriately for the man's lifestyle sends the message, *I am wife material.* Men marry women they perceive as situational virgins who move easily in their world.

➤ If you want to marry a man who is more attractive than you, try for a very good-looking one. He is more likely to find attributes other than physical beauty irresistible.

➤ Enlisting your man's support in making a good first impression on his family increases your chance of marrying him.

3

Women Men Marry

THERE ARE WOMEN in today's world who never worry about falling in love or getting married. Most of them live in societies where marriages are arranged. Their fathers make all their life-shaping decisions before they marry, and their husbands make them afterward. They also do not have to worry about getting an education, succeeding in a career, or even driving a car, because those are not realistic options. They live limited lives with limited freedom.

No American woman I have ever met would trade her freedoms for such a life. Still, with freedom and choices come risks, the most obvious one being you might never marry. Life in a free society with all its options is a bit of a gamble. The purpose of this chapter is to make finding a husband, if not a sure thing, less of a gamble.

Friends in Need

Who is a single woman's best ally in finding a mate? Oddly enough, it's other women. Here are a few facts to consider.

The first thing we learned from women coming out of marriage license bureaus was that they had a large number of female friends, most of whom were about the same age; they were newly married, engaged, or single but looking.

- ➤ When we asked the women to tell us with whom they had spent most of their time during the past five years, most named from five to eleven single women.

- ➤ Ninety-two percent of these brides-to-be came from the same socioeconomic background as a majority of their friends.

- ➤ Most of those in their twenties and early thirties also had a close circle of three to six friends.

- ➤ They spent three-quarters of their leisure time in the company of these friends.

- ➤ These engaged women were members of several loosely organized groups, which often overlapped.

- ➤ More than 90 percent of them had between seven and fourteen female friends.

- ➤ The vast majority of single women we interviewed coming out of marriage license bureaus worked with two or three single women with whom they also socialized.

- ➤ They also had five or six women in their neighborhood with whom they were friendly, and from three to six longtime friends, often school chums, with whom they regularly spent time.

- ➤ Most had one or two best friends, women close to their own age.

The second thing those in their twenties and thirties had in common was that before their engagement, they had gone with their girlfriends to singles places to meet men. Their hangouts had ranged from singles bars in New York City to church functions in small Southern towns.

The advantages of these associations to a single woman was obvious. When these women threw parties, they invited friends—male friends. This ensured that they met more single men than the women who had fewer girlfriends. In addition, they went out of their way to set each other up. They often invited eligible men to dinner or other gatherings and introduced the men to their friends. Some women enjoy playing matchmaker and do it regularly. Occasionally it works, and the two people brought together become a couple. Even when that does not happen, the woman benefits by expanding her social circle.

The women in these groups were not involved in a conspiracy whose sole purpose was to find men—they really were friends. They didn't spend all their spare time looking for husbands. If they lived on their own, they usually took turns cooking for each other. They were also likely to go to dinner, to the theater, and shopping together. We found groups of women who exercised together at the same gym or went walking or running together. Since one of their primary interests was finding The One, they sought out single men together and supported each other in this endeavor. This was especially true in the case of close friends.

When we contrasted these women with the ones who were forty and older and admitted they didn't have any immediate prospects of getting married, we found the older group had far fewer single female friends. At first, I thought that this was simply a function of age; I figured most of their single friends had married, and now they had only two or three unmarried friends with whom they associated.

But that didn't prove to be the whole truth, although it was a factor. We found when we questioned the women in their forties about the number of friends they'd had when they were in their twenties, it was far fewer, on average, than the women who were about to marry. So the first thing you should do if you want to find a man to marry is to make friends with women.

Male Friends Are Not Helpful

Surprisingly, the women coming out of marriage license bureaus didn't have more male friends than the women who were forty and unmarried had had when they were their age. When the unattached forty-year-old women were in their twenties, they had about the same number of male friends as the engaged women had. The number of male friends they had did not, in any meaningful way, seem to influence their chances of getting married. At first this appears to fly in the face of common sense, because women often marry men who start out as friends, but statistically it didn't seem to make a great deal of difference.

After speaking to thirty-seven single men who had a number of female friends, I concluded that the reason these friendships did not significantly increase a woman's chance of marrying was that the men almost never went out of their way to introduce their female friends to other men. That just isn't something men do.

My Best Friend's Wedding?

Another characteristic of women who marry was that like the men we studied, they often married around the same time as their friends. It seems that when half a dozen young women hang out together and one or two get married, the others quickly follow. We followed nine groups of four to seven single women after one or two members of the groups became engaged. Within two years, at least half the others were married or engaged.

The women told us there are a number of reasons for this. The primary reason is these women feel they're being left behind and start putting pressure on their boyfriends, or start looking more seriously for a man to marry. Once one or two women in one of these groups marry, the chance that others will follow suit within a year or two increases dramatically. Within four years, most of the other women in the group will become engaged or married.

We questioned unmarried women in the forty-plus group about this phenomenon and found that many had girlfriends who got married when they were in their early- or mid-thirties. They told us that they felt pressure to get married when their friends did, but did not have as many opportunities. Suddenly they found it was much harder to meet eligible men without the help of their friends who were now married and had different concerns.

If you are in your twenties, you increase your chances of marrying if your girlfriends get engaged in their twenties.

When this phenomenon caught my attention, I ran several focus groups with single women who were in their midthirties whose friends had just married. They found themselves in a very unusual position. A number of them said that they went from having a full social life to being very lonely in the blink of an eye. As one woman put it, she woke up one morning and realized it was no longer fun or even all right to be stuck in the singles scene. The female friends who used to invite them to parties and arrange for them to meet men were married and had other concerns. At least half the women who hit thirty became very determined to marry, and around 30 percent of these determined women did marry or become engaged within three years. So take note!

If you reach thirty and want to get married, reorganize your life to make finding a husband your primary goal for the next two to three years. No matter what your educational background or your professional accomplishments, finding a husband becomes more difficult once you are no longer circulating on the singles scene.

Don't make the mistake of thinking there are still many men available just because you see men wandering around unmarried in their late thirties and early forties. Scores of women who reached thirty-six told us the men they knew in that age range were dating and marrying women in their twenties. After interviewing hundreds of single women in their forties:

If I were to pick the age at which a woman should put extra effort into finding a husband, it would be twenty-eight. Time is your enemy.

Choosing Career Over Marriage

Sometimes it's a clear-cut choice. We interviewed several hundred women in their late thirties and forties who were unmarried and didn't have immediate prospects of getting married. About one in three told us they weren't married because they had sacrificed their social life for their careers. Most said they regretted making that choice—despite the fact that it had been a conscious decision, and at the time they had intellectually accepted the idea that they might never marry.

Gina, a professional woman from a large Midwestern city, told us that when she was in her twenties, she had decided to pass on a social life and possibly even on a husband. She thought she might marry later on, but she wasn't particularly upset about living on her own. Gina explained that she had no real desire to have children, unlike some of her friends who did marry. She thought the desire to have children was the reason many of her friends married, rather than that they were dying to live with a man.

When we talked to Gina, she was forty-four and very successful. She told us she wasn't lonely; her career kept her busy—she happily worked twelve hours a day—and she had many friends at work. But now, Gina said, she missed having someone with whom to share her victories. When she was in her twenties and thirties, she enjoyed sharing her advances, having someone with whom to celebrate when she made a big business move. Now, she said regretfully, she doesn't have anyone who cheers with her and shares her accomplishments.

Her complaint was not atypical. Most of the women over forty we interviewed wanted to get married for the companionship, so they would have someone with whom to share their lives. Most believed they were missing out by not having a special man in their lives.

Not for Everyone

Around 70 percent of the successful single career women in their forties and fifties we talked to believed that a young woman who gives up marriage and a husband for her career will probably regret it. Around 20 percent of successful single women, however, are happy with their lives and would not change if they had the chance. About half of these women said they were attracted to men but did not think marriage was for them. They liked their independence too much to have to answer to anyone.

Marriage is not for everyone. After talking to hundreds of single men and women, I'm convinced there are people who aren't suited for marriage, and they often decide correctly to remain single.

Engineering Women Have the Time of Their Lives

The real career trip isn't trading that little gold band for the gold ring on the professional merry-go-round. The percentage of successful career women who never marry is only slightly higher than the percentage of unmarried women in the general population. When we looked in corporations, we found that most of the successful women had husbands and children. Interestingly, these women said the difference between them and the women who didn't marry was planning. They went about getting a husband the same way they went about succeeding in their careers. The women very carefully allocated their time when they were single so that they had a social life. Only occasionally, they told us, did they have to put their careers ahead of their social life, and when they did they tried to work harder to make up for it.

For example, two executive women told us about having to give up a great singles weekend at the beach to attend a business conference. They made it a point to arrange for dates when they got back. They didn't let their business life control their social life—nor did they allow their social life to interfere with success in the workplace.

We ran several different focus groups dealing with career and marriage. The first group was composed of women in their early forties who were not married, the second of women in their early forties who had married, most of whom had children, and the third was a mixed group. All the women in these groups had similar backgrounds and careers. The women who were not married basically concurred with the answers in the survey. Most admitted they had not really worked at having a social life when they were younger. They had let their careers dominate their lives when they were in their twenties and thirties, and by the time they decided they wanted to marry, meeting men was much more difficult.

We started the focus group with the married career women by summarizing for them the comments of the unmarried career women. To give them a concrete idea of what was discussed, I had them look at highlights of a videotape of the single women's session before asking them to comment. During the session, the single women explained that it was impossible for them to function in their positions and still have an active social life.

One was an attorney. She said that when she had an important case—especially when she was involved in a trial—she worked sixteen hours a day. In addition, from a couple of days to a couple of months before going into court, she had time for little else.

Another of the unmarried women was an engineer. She explained that the nature of her job made dating very difficult. When her division got a big contract, everybody worked long hours, including weekends, until it was over. Then they all kicked back. As a reward, the boss let her and her fellow engineers leave after lunch for a few weeks. But being off Tuesday afternoons at two o'clock, she pointed out, didn't do much to enhance her social life.

Another woman's story was a replay of the tale told by half a dozen women in management. She complained that between the long hours at work and other obligations, she had very little time for socializing.

The married women's reaction to the comments of their unmarried counterparts was one of disbelief. A married attorney said of the unmarried attorney that her facts were correct, but she wasn't being entirely truthful: "I'd love to cross-examine her. I'm in the same business. There are times when you're very busy and times when you're not. You have to do some planning." When she had downtime in her single days, she told us, she went out almost every night. Two women who were engineers said basically the same thing. Both had not only dated male engineers but had also gone together to singles places. These engineering women agreed that when they weren't working hard, they were playing hard.

Finally, one of the women stood up and made a little speech. "We're businesswomen," she began. "Let's approach this the way we'd deal with a problem at work. The unmarried career woman has two challenges. First, she has to learn to manage her time. When she's not working twelve hours a day, she shouldn't be spending her time shopping for her business wardrobe, cleaning her apartment, doing her nails, or anything else she can hire people to do for her. She should be making an effort to meet single men. That would be the most efficient use of her time.

"Second, I'm sure we'd all agree she needs to associate with women in a similar position. If she's going to lunch every day with the married women in her office, she's making a mistake. She should lunch with single women who might go out after work."

Several of the participants agreed that one of the big problems of the successful single career woman is that she finds herself socializing with people who are older and married. In addition, since most single people go out on Friday and Saturday nights, she should arrange her schedule so she can be free on weekends as often as possible.

They also advised single career women to seek out friends who are in similar businesses and economic positions and can afford to do the things they want to do. One woman explained that while she had money, her friends had more time. Still, she could afford to throw a series of small dinner parties to meet men, while they could not. Another executive told the group she often asked her girlfriends to go out Friday nights, but they preferred to stay home and do their nails or hair. Since her free time was at a premium, she wanted to use all of it. She did not drop her old friends, but she did find new ones— women with high-powered careers like hers and similar needs. Once she took that step, her social life improved dramatically.

Several women in the session agreed that having friends with similar problems was one of the secrets to having a successful career and social life.

Most of the very successful women suggested that the single women change their priorities. Two married women said when they were in their twenties and found themselves working in businesses with few if any eligible men, they quit and found other jobs. A number of women in the married group pointed out that this was not always practical. The group's final solution was a compromise. They recommended that when a woman finds herself working in a position where meeting eligible men is next to impossible, she should look at the possibility of changing jobs, but if that isn't possible, she must adjust her work schedule to increase her chances of meeting men. You not only have to go where men are, but you have to go *when* they are there.

The interesting thing is that while women talk about the choice between marriage and a career all the time, we met only three who said they'd consciously made this choice. Most of those who maintained that the demands of their careers interfered with their finding husbands admitted that they had sacrificed their social lives one day at a time. Several told our researchers that they woke up one day and realized it was too late—they were probably never going to marry. A number of them complained that their youth seemed to fly by, but they were not typical. More than 80 percent of the successful married career women we interviewed observed that when they were single, they were acutely aware of every birthday. They knew they had a limited time to find a husband, and with that in mind put great effort into meeting eligible men.

When You Can't Fish Off the Company Pier

The women who really have a problem with their careers are those who work in fields where there are few if any eligible men. Among the unmarried women in their forties we interviewed, we found that a substantial percentage worked in businesses where they hardly ever met men. We talked to three women in the fashion industry, for example, who claimed there were few eligible men where they worked. Most of their male colleagues were either married or gay. For these women, it was a real problem, and one for which I have no solution except to suggest finding a new career path or putting a lot more energy into their social life outside of work. Yes, easier said than done. While it's a problem, however, it's not insoluble.

The first group of unmarried women in their forties we interviewed lived in Boston. They complained that in their field most of the men were gay or married. When several weeks later we ran across the same complaint in San Francisco and in six other large cities, we realized it was a major issue. Working in industries with a large number of gay men was an obstacle for some women, but for others it turned out to be more of an excuse than an insoluble problem. About half the women we interviewed coming out of marriage license bureaus met few or any eligible men at work. They said they made up for that by trying harder outside the workplace.

Working odd hours made it very difficult for women to meet men. Women whose jobs required them to work weekends and irregular shifts made up an inordinately large percentage of the unmarried women we interviewed, and many of them thought that this was one of the reasons they had never married. When they worked 4 P.M. to midnight and then went out, everyone else had been partying for hours and looked foolish and unappealing to them. The women who worked graveyard shifts said they had to leave when the party was just getting started. When we compared unmarried women who worked odd hours to married women who did likewise, however, we found that while both groups had the same complaints, they handled them differently. The married women went to parties—even when they knew they would not be able to stay long—and made the best of a bad situation.

You've Worked All Your Life for This?

The most surprising finding was that the largest group of women who let their jobs kill their social lives didn't have even moderately successful careers. Often they were women in dead-end jobs. One woman was a housemother in a private school in a small town in Connecticut, where no men were available to her nine months of the year. To make matters worse, during the other three months she worked in a girls' camp in the Maine woods. She had no social life. Believe it or not, her story was not that unusual. Her complaints about being trapped by life were very similar to dozens of other women's tales.

One young woman, Sara, worked as a typist for a résumé service. She got up in the morning, got dressed, walked down the street to her office, and sat at a computer in a back room typing for eight hours. The other three women in the office were all in their sixties. Sara told us men came into the reception area, but she never met them. She had been hired by the typing service out of high school, and stayed in the job for eleven years. That limited not only the number of men she met but also the number of single women with whom she associated.

I recommend—and my researchers unanimously agree:

No woman should ever work at a job where she does not meet and make friends with men and women of her own age.

If she stays in such a position, she dramatically decreases the chances that she will marry. Ironically, most of the women we talked to who had such jobs didn't care much about them. When we asked them at age forty why they had stayed, a majority gave one of two answers: they didn't know, or they were used to the job and did not like change. They were in what the female researchers called "the unmarried rut."

If you are in an unmarried rut, don't wait until next week, get out of it this week. Don't think about it, do it. It is the worst of all possible situations.

Where the Boys Are

Research shows that women who go to great lengths to seek out the company of single men are more likely to marry than women who do not. The women we interviewed coming out of marriage license bureaus said that before they met Mr. Right, they went out of their way to be around single men; for instance, more than 40 percent looked for jobs where they would encounter single men. These women were more likely than the women who did not marry to take vacations where they would meet single men, to join clubs with single men as members, and to go to places where single men congregated.

These proactive women understood that finding the right man was not a matter of attracting tons of men, because you have to attract only one. It was clear to the women that it was a numbers game.

Dating Mr. Wrong, believe it or not, helps. The women we met who were about to marry dated more frequently than those who never married. They were more likely to go out with men they would never consider marrying than women who did not marry.

Throughout the study, we ran the results by our researchers and a cross section of those we had surveyed. If we were unable to speak to the same respondents who took the survey, we found people who matched them as closely as possible. This was our standard procedure, because often, when the people surveyed heard the results, they were convinced they were inaccurate, or at least misleading, and often they were right. Most often, misunderstanding arose because of a misinterpretation of their answers to our questions. In this case, we had assumed that women who said they put great effort into meeting eligible men were telling the unvarnished truth. We saw no reason for them to lie. The young women we interviewed disagreed.

After the women coming out of marriage license bureaus challenged our conclusions that the single women had accurately relayed their experiences, we decided to interview groups of women in New York City. The brides-to-be maintained that while most women gave lip service to meeting single men, it was not a top priority for many. They suggested that many of the women we interviewed were describing the world as they would like it to be, not as it was. To prove how wrong we were, two women agreed to accompany us as we interviewed groups of single women for the second time. One of the first groups we interviewed was at the Metropolitan Museum in New York City. They claimed one of the reasons they were at the museum was that it would be a good place to meet a nice man. But under questioning from the two women accompanying us, they admitted that single men do not hang out in museums. This group of five women also told us they knew that men hung out in sports bars when big games are being played. They also confessed they had never been to a sports bar, and three of the five insisted they would never go to one. I am not suggesting that women should go to sports bars every time a big game is on TV. Both the brides-to-be accompanying us and the women being interviewed, however, agreed that if you want to meet men, you have to pick a place where men really go.

Women who marry make a special effort to seek the company of eligible men. Apparently, most women put some effort into meeting men, but there is no doubt that those who marry are more persistent and realistic than those who do not. When we asked engaged women and single women (who had no immediate marriage prospects) to describe where and how often they had sought out the company of men when they were in their early twenties, we saw two major differences:

➤ Women who were about to marry participated in masculine activities in which they had no real interest three times as often as women who remained single.

➤ The engaged women were almost twice as likely to have made major sacrifices in their lifestyles—even changing jobs or moving to a new place—so they could meet eligible men.

Girls, Have Fun!

Women who marry have more fun when they are single than those who don't. They date more often, they party more, they play more, and they have more boyfriends. This is not because they are more popular—we factored personal popularity into our research. You can best see the difference by how they answered the cruise ship question. If they said they had been on a cruise ship, we asked them to describe exactly how they spent their time.

When I was in my midtwenties, I worked as a bartender on cruise ships. I noticed that on the first night, many of the young women stayed in their cabins and did their hair, pressed their clothing, and so forth. They were often the same women who did not go ashore in the afternoon and instead prepared for a dance or some other activity that night. Other young women went everywhere and did everything. The young crew members referred to the two groups as "goers" and "gooers." The goers were game to go everywhere, while the gooers were always putting on goo, getting ready for hours on end. We liked the goers, and apparently so do most men, because they were far more likely to marry.

Putting Princesshood Behind You

Women with unreasonable expectations often do not marry. Unreasonable expectations of men and marriage come from three sources. The first we refer to as "Daddy is a doctor, lawyer, or Indian chief." The lifestyle of some young women is based on their father's income, and it is hard to give this up for a young man who cannot duplicate that lifestyle. If a young woman thinks that way, the chances that she will remain single are very high. But at least she is making a conscious choice between lifestyles. Many women who have unrealistic goals are not hanging on to a better lifestyle but holding out for a dream.

We ran across the first and most obvious example of trading reality for dreams when we interviewed several unmarried women in their forties and fifties who worked for a large metropolitan hospital. They lived in apartments in a nurses' residence that they called "Menopause Manor." (I know the women we interviewed weren't unusual because my wife, Maureen, was a nurse, and when she was young, she and her friends also referred to their nurses' residence as "Menopause Manor.")

Nurses meet a great number of men, both single and married. They have extended friendships and contacts, and I'm sure a very high percentage marry. Those who remain single in many cases had worked with doctors and decided they wanted to marry a doctor—*only* a doctor. A number of these women went out of their way to let us know they would marry if they found a doctor they liked. This comment was made by four or five nurses in their late forties or early fifties who were hanging on to their unrealistic expectations.

If these women had not married a doctor by the time they were forty-five, the chances they would marry one were about the same as hitting the lottery. We ran across the same unrealistic attitude when we interviewed several single secretaries in Washington who insisted they were holding out for a congressman or senator.

If you work for or around rich and/or powerful men and find yourself thinking you have to marry one of them, you are on the way to becoming your own worst enemy. Better yet, look at the reality—what kind of husbands do these men make? Would the demands of the job (and the temptation of having women flocking around them) make for a happy marriage?

Take a deep breath and start dating men you have a real chance of marrying and who would make good husbands.

When Friends and Family Say No

While a woman with high expectations can be her own worst enemy, much of the time unrealistic expectations are imposed on her by others. Many have a friend or parent who believes that she should only marry a man who has attained a certain level of success. These people are so important or dominant in her life that she runs all the men she dates past them. She brings the man home, where he is accepted or rejected by Mom or Dad, or she takes him out on a date and introduces him to her friends, who insist that she only marry a millionaire. These advisers invariably describe almost every young man as a loser, which leaves the young woman, if she accepts their definition, with no one to marry.

This is all too common. When we interviewed the people in these women's lives who were making these decisions, we found that in many case they were oblivious to the effects of their meddling. Some of them, particularly the mothers, were shocked when we told them they were limiting their daughter's choice of men. More than one became annoyed, and a few were outraged when we even mentioned the possibility. But it's a simple fact.

Among the unmarried women in their forties and fifties, we found a number who'd had several chances to marry but had turned the man down because someone close to them did not accept him. Most of the women in their fifties regretted having let others rule their lives. Some were quite bitter about it, even though in their hearts they realized it was their decision. The irony was that the decision makers more often than not married someone they would have rejected for their daughter or friend.

Every woman should have standards, and she shouldn't marry someone who fails to live up to those standards—but the standards should be hers, and they should be based in reality. No one else, no matter how well-meaning, can decide whom you should marry. After interviewing several hundred women, I am also convinced that standards should not be carved in stone. No one should have a litmus test for a prospective mate.

Janet had a litmus test that almost got in the way of a good relationship. A very successful attorney in one of our focus groups, she told us she had decided she would never marry a man who didn't have a college degree. So when Henry, a man she knew from high school, called her, Janet had her roommate tell him she wasn't home. But Henry didn't discourage easily; he called at least once a year. When he did catch her, she always turned him down, politely but very firmly. He should have gotten the message: She just wasn't interested in seeing him.

Janet then related how God had smiled at her. One day, before she could hang up, Henry shouted, "Wait, I'm not asking you out. I've given up on dating you. I'm being sued. I need an attorney, and you're the only one I know and trust." He swore it was strictly business, and she agreed to see him to discuss his case.

When she'd graduated from high school, Janet was convinced that anybody who didn't go to college was stupid.

Henry had been one of the dumb jocks who never studied, and she had vowed she'd never marry someone like him. After high school he went to work as a car salesman, and in five years he owned his own dealership. Fifteen years later, as Janet found out to her amazement when he came to see her about the lawsuit, he owned several dealerships, an apartment house complex, and several office buildings. He was the richest and most successful car dealer in the state, and he could have bought and sold Janet's entire law firm.

The eighteen-million-dollar lawsuit, as it turned out, was not as much of a threat as he had feared; Janet was able to reassure him that his insurance company would defend him. She also discovered that she enjoyed his company. They began dating, and one thing led to another. When he proposed some months later, she said yes and explained why she had not gone out with him. "Well, if that's all you wanted," he retorted, "I'll pick up my degree in my spare time." He had already taken all the business courses necessary for graduation and had audited about half those needed for a master's in business administration. If it would make her happy, Henry said, he would start next semester. Janet said there was no need.

Real Men Are Attracted to Talented Women

The men coming out of marriage license bureaus bragged about their future wives' talents and accomplishments. When I discussed this finding with my researchers, most of whom were very well-educated women, I discovered they found it hard to believe. They claimed their experiences had taught them that men were intimidated by talented women. They didn't think the men we had talked to had any reason to lie, but they remained skeptical. One of the researchers suggested we take a second look at the men who had made those statements.

The first thing we noticed was that the men who bragged about the accomplishments of their women were generally macho guys, bursting with self-confidence. Several had very good reasons: Two had started very successful firms, another was a successful lawyer, while a fourth, at age forty-two, had become a vice president of a large company. What made it a little tricky is that one in three displayed this self-assurance without any apparent reason. Several of the researchers said they could tell these were men with tremendous egos, but they admitted they couldn't spot which men would react that way. The only thing the researchers agreed on was that if a woman meets a man who is proud of his accomplishments, whatever they are, she should be proud of hers, too.

Living on Your Own

Women often think of men who live with their parents as being Mama's boys, or less mature than men who live on their own. There is a degree of truth in this, but:

It's more important for a woman to live on her own than it is for a man.

This doesn't mean she has to have her own place; she can share with another single woman. Women often do this, and it's a good idea for safety and just for sociability (not to mention the saving on living costs). The more female friends you have, as noted earlier, the more likely you are to run into eligible men.

Women who live with their parents, for reasons I can only guess, are much less likely to marry than women who live independently. Possibly it is because parents put restrictions on what a woman does when she is in her early twenties—going away for weekends, staying out all night, partying until four o'clock in the morning. This probably reduces her chances of being intimate with a man and interferes in other ways with a relationship's development. I'm not sure what the reason is, but it is a statistical truth that if you live at home, you are less likely to marry than if you live on your own.

Size Matters

Women who are slender have better odds of marrying. Being overweight dramatically reduces your chances of attracting and marrying men. That's a tough one to accept, but it's a simple statistical fact. Naturally, there are many overweight women who do marry. We ran across dozens. But when we talked to women in their twenties and thirties, we found that those who were overweight dated less, had sex less often, were less likely to have steady boyfriends, and were less likely to marry than their svelte sisters. I hesitate to mention this because I'm constantly reading and hearing about women dieting to the point of illness or even death. Just a few years ago, the fashion industry was pushing "concentration camp chic." The models in the ads, whom young women often try to imitate, looked starved and sickly. Men are not attracted to sickly.

If you're overweight, according to the standards for age and build endorsed by the American Heart Association, I suggest you talk to your doctor about undertaking a diet and exercise regimen.

The weight issue is a harsh reality when it comes to who marries most, but it is a reality, and I feel obligated to report it.

Personal Appearance

Women who pay attention to their personal appearance are more likely to attract men than women who do not. We found there was a marked difference between women who married and women who didn't in the way they cared for themselves. It is a statistical fact that the women who marry are more likely to spend time in a salon getting their hair and nails done than women who do not. One reason for this is that there is no one element in appearance that tends to attract men more than others. I can't prove it, because a woman's attractiveness is a matter of individual opinion. I am firmly convinced, however, that if a fairly attractive woman puts real effort into looking her best, she is more likely to attract men than a woman who is slightly better looking but doesn't put that same effort into keeping up her appearance. Most of the female researchers agreed.

The Greatest Aphrodisiac: Love Yourself

We have found that women with high self-esteem don't love men who do not love them. Self-confident women were far more successful with men than women who admitted they continued to love men who did not love them. Women who doted on men who obviously didn't care about them were in most cases treated shabbily.

Interestingly, these unmarried women often spoke of the men who had dumped them in glowing terms, while married or engaged women often referred to men who broke up with them as "losers." The single women often made the men who did not reciprocate their feelings the center of their universe. More than one expressed regret that she did not measure up to what the man she adored expected. The married and engaged women were, in most cases, the centers of their own universes and did not measure themselves by the standards of a man who rejected them. Rather, the women measured the men by their own standards. Men who made them happy were winners, and men who failed to do so were losers.

So if you find yourself stuck on a guy who does not return your affections, pry yourself loose and move on. Do whatever it takes to boost your self-esteem and improve your life. Then focus on dating men who are truly interested in you.

Date Only Eligible Men

There is another way to increase your chances of getting married—do not go out with married men. To begin with, it's wrong. Any woman who breaks up a family, given all the research on what divorce does not only to the adults involved but also to the children, is making a grave mistake.

Dating married men is not smart. If you go out with a married man who lives with his wife, the chances are slim that he will leave her. If he has not left her within three months of meeting you, the likelihood goes down to almost zero. We met at least a dozen women who spent years of their youth dating a married man who was always "about" to get divorced. These married cheaters are another type of stringer—a multiple stringer. He strings along his often unknowing wife as well as his lover or lovers. He strings women along and never delivers.

There is one more *big* reason not to go out with a married man. If he marries you after cheating on his wife, he is very likely to cheat on you, too.

The women researchers who interviewed these people were of two opinions. The first group said that women who went out with married men and got stuck had it coming. They were doing something ethically wrong, and they could not expect to be rewarded for their actions.

The other group said that these women were the biggest fools in the world. The researchers interviewed women who had been the "other woman" most of their adult lives. Once they became the other woman, their social lives stopped. They didn't date; they didn't have a normal relationship with their married lover; they spent a lot of time hiding. About half these women, under pressure from a man who would not give up his wife, gave up their friends. They admitted to sitting around waiting for the few minutes that the married man would spend with them. Women who date married men usually have sad and wasted lives. It almost invariably leaves the woman unhappy.

One woman, after having been inspired in a focus group to describe her life as it really was, took out her cell phone and broke up with a married man she had been dating for two years. Several others who had volunteered to answer questions about their love lives found it so painful they broke off the interviews in tears. We could locate only sixteen women dating married men who would talk to us, even after we told them we would sign nondisclosure agreements (a contract that guarantees substantial payment if their identities are ever revealed). Not one said she was happy with her life.

It May Seem Obvious, But . . .

Do not go out with gay men. We met a number of unmarried women in their forties who had gay male friends who filled in as escorts when needed. It was very convenient, and it helped them through long periods without dating. But several women said that if they had not relied on their gay friends, they would have been forced to seek the company of eligible men. Looking back, they regretted that they had not. A number of women admitted that going out with gay men when you are over forty is a tacit admission that you aren't looking.

Second Chances

One of the most intriguing things we discovered when interviewing brides coming out of marriage license bureaus is that about 20 percent didn't like their husband when they first met him. Some had known their husbands in high school; they told us that he had been a motorcycle bum or a nerd or a dumb jock, and they wouldn't even consider going out with him. This was a big problem, because they often assumed that at twenty-eight, twenty-nine, or thirty he'd still be the same person.

A second group of brides told us that the first time they met their husband, they couldn't stand him. Others told us after one or two dates, they had decided he was not for them and dropped him. What made these men different was that they kept coming back. They kept asking for dates. They called six months later to ask what was happening. They were obviously thinking of the woman. And the woman—because she had not had a date in a while, or because she got tired of saying no—relented and accepted the date. These women discovered that the second time around was much better than the first.

There was a fine line between those men who kept coming back and stalkers. When I asked the women if they were ever afraid the persistent suitor was stalking them, they said no; he never threatened them or made them feel uncomfortable. They said they'd be happy to have him as a neighbor, just not as a lover. In most cases, they did not go from disliking to liking him, they went from liking him one way to liking him another way.

Our women researchers were astounded at the percentage of women who had disliked the man they were marrying when they had first met. They were also surprised by how often these relationships worked out. A number of the researchers had similar men in their lives and were ignoring them. Several had dated a man years ago who called them year after year and simply would not take no for an answer. A few of our researchers, after reviewing the interviews, decided to go out with a guy they had turned down several times.

This tactic worked for at least one of our researchers. Old flames who didn't light your fire in the past may do so today. After taking a second look, however, most women decide they were right the first time. Nevertheless, if you just didn't click the first time, there's a real chance you might on the second, particularly if the dates are more than a year apart. So don't be afraid to give a guy a second chance—it just might improve your chances of getting married.

Several women and men coming out of marriage license bureaus told us love can happen the second or even the third time around. It did for one in nine women coming out of marriage license bureaus.

Women Men Marry, Statistically Speaking

➤ Women with a large number of female friends are more likely to marry than women with a larger number of male friends.

➤ Many unmarried women over forty who choose to sacrifice their social lives for their career when they're young regret making that choice later.

➤ The secret to having a successful career *and* a marriage is time management.

➤ The larger the number of single men and women with whom you work, the greater your chances of marrying.

➤ Women with unrealistic expectations often remain single.

➤ Self-confident men are attracted to accomplished, self-assured, and talented women.

➤ Women who waste their time with stringers or with men who don't care for them hurt their chances of marrying.

➤ Men and women who have their own places are more likely to marry.

➤ Being slender attracts more men, therefore increasing your chances of marrying.

> Women who put effort into looking their best are more likely to marry than those who don't.

> It's better to be a goer than a gooer—find a quick, easy beauty regimen and then get out there and go.

> Women who go out a second or even a third time with men they are not crazy about at first often end up happily married to them.

> Women who put real effort into seeking out the company of single men are more likely to marry than those who do not.

> Women who have active social lives are more likely to marry than those who don't.

4

The Stages in a Relationship

AFTER QUESTIONING 410 men and 376 women, the team came to the conclusion that while there was no step-by-step plan that successful couples follow, there were identifiable stages in most relationships. We also discovered we could usually tell if the relationship was likely to lead to marriage, based on these stages.

Enter, Stage One: Living Up to Expectations

The first stage in a relationship can best be described as living up to expectations. When a man asks a woman out, it's usually because he thinks she's the type of woman with whom he connects—for instance, not assertive and not very sophisticated. If after one or two dates he discovers that she is very assertive and sophisticated, he probably will never call again. Men believe that within five minutes they can size up most women by the way they look and sound. Research showed that this was not so: They were wrong more often than they were right.

If women understood this, perhaps their feelings wouldn't be so easily hurt when a man doesn't call, because in most cases it's simply a tacit admission that he made a mistake. He thought the woman would act and think one way, and she acted and thought another.

Stage Two:
Getting to Know You

We discovered seven significant differences between women who were usually asked for second, third, and fourth dates and those who weren't:

> ➤ The women who were asked for follow-up dates were more likely to have dated extensively while in school.

> ➤ These women have long-standing relationships with male friends, or have brothers. They have a better understanding of men than the women who did not get follow-up dates.

> ➤ The women who had repeat dates were less concerned with impressing their dates than with having a good time. As a result, they were better company.

> ➤ These women almost never had sex on the first date.

> ➤ They usually went along with the man's plans, but when they disapproved of something, they were up front about their objections. Several dozen women at marriage license bureaus said on the first date their fiancés came on too strong, and they objected in no uncertain terms.

> ➤ These women were friendly and positive.

➤ They were a good audience. They listened to what their date said and showed an interest in him or concern about his welfare. There is no way of overestimating the importance of showing interest in a man or concern about his welfare.

Specific Acts of Kindness

We had one prospective groom after another tell us that when early in their relationship his fiancée showed she was concerned about his health, career, or future, he started seeing her as someone he should take seriously. This concern was displayed in a number of ways. Several of these men told us they had a physical problem—a cold or flu, and in one case a sprained ankle—and their future bride in some way, usually very minor, took care of them, providing aspirin or cold tablets, or insisting they rest until they felt better.

Dave told us when he first met his future fiancée, Annie, at a mutual friend's house, she asked him if he felt okay. He assured her several times that he felt fine, but she put her hand on his forehead and said, "You should be in bed." When Dave gave Annie a lecherous grin, she said, "Idiot, you're burning up." After a short conversation, she agreed to drive him home. Dave went along only because he was hoping to make a pass at her, but he got nowhere. Annie walked him into his parents' house and told them he had a fever and they had better put him to bed. Annie added that he was just as big an idiot as her brother and would probably go out again after she left and get pneumonia. Dave's parents and his two sisters thanked her, and she left.

From that evening on, all his sisters could talk about was his dating "that Annie girl." When Dave explained he did not remember her last name or have her telephone number, one of his sisters located it for him. When he called, Annie did not remember Dave at first. As soon as he described himself as the idiot with a fever, Annie remembered him but refused to date him. It was only after he explained that his sisters would not let up until he went out with her that Annie agreed to go out with Dave—once.

I met them almost two years later coming out of a marriage license bureau. Annie told us she went out with Dave more than once because he acted like a gentlemen and not a jerk the second time they met. Dave explained he was polite because she had taken him home when she had no interest in him and had made it clear she thought he was an idiot. In his mind, that made her very special. Her concern was expressed before their first date, but it could have become apparent anytime in the early stages of this relationship and had the same results.

Several men said that when they started dating the woman they eventually would marry, the subject of going back to school, taking career training, or trying for a better job came up in conversation. When it did, the women encouraged their future husbands to do whatever it took to improve. They said that even before they had a relationship, they knew their fiancées had their best interests at heart, and that made them special.

Concern can be shown in minor ways. One soon-to-be-married man said he was impressed when his fiancée canceled their second date after discovering that he had an important meeting in the morning. And then there was Steve, who was impressed when his future fiancée, Faye, talked him out of taking her to the most expensive restaurant in town on their first date. Faye's argument was that no meal was worth what that place charged. Steve owned his own company and could easily afford the meals he ate there regularly, but Faye was the first woman ever to try to discourage him from spending money on her. So clearly, showing this type of concern for a man early on would be a wise thing to do!

Why Didn't He Call?

We also asked men why they didn't call a woman back after two or more dates. More than half said they weren't sure. The answer we heard most often was something to the effect that there was no chemistry. I included in this group answers such as "We didn't get along," "Things didn't work out the way I thought they would," and so forth. When we asked them to be more specific, most of the men couldn't. Fifty-four percent said there was nothing wrong with the woman they dated, and a handful added, without being asked, that she would probably be perfect for someone else.

We concluded that asking why a man didn't call was a meaningless question as far as most men are concerned. As men see it, they need a reason to call again—because it could lead to other things—but they do not need a reason not to call.

Another common reason for not calling in the getting-to-know-you phase was that women started getting too serious too soon. Of the men we questioned, 23 percent told us they had been on a first or second date within the last year with a woman who started talking about their relationship as if they were already a couple. A few women during these introductory dates started planning their futures together. Several women actually asked their dates how many kids they would like to have.

In some cases, it may have been the woman's way of ending

the relationship. One of the standard jokes female comics tell is, "How do you get rid of a man? Simple. Tell him you love him and you want to have his children." Like most good jokes, it contains a grain of truth. Dozens of men reported that within the last year a woman, after only one or two dates, began to talk as though she was envisioning a permanent relationship, and that caused the man to drop her like a hot potato. Five said it made them so uncomfortable they ended the date early. Getting too serious too quickly is one of the worst mistakes a woman can make.

If men react this way, it is not necessarily because they are afraid of commitment. Several of the men who recounted these stories were interviewed coming out of marriage license bureaus.

A common reason men gave for not calling was that the woman had turned out not to be as positive as they had thought. When they first met she was friendly and upbeat, but after one or two dates they decided she had been putting on an act. They told our researchers that the women started making negative comments about places they went, people they knew, and other women, and this annoyed the men. When talking to other women, women sometimes make catty comments about other women. But this is a mistake when talking to a man—nine out of ten men find catty remarks a turnoff.

Such apparent personality changes after a first encounter can take a variety of forms. About half a dozen men told us the women they met were nice and quiet to begin with, but as soon as they started dating, they became loud and abrasive. The women were either pretending to be refined, or they were bashful, and once they relaxed, they let undesirable qualities take over.

Women should also know that men gave a whole set of reasons for not calling that had more to do with the men than the women. They told our researchers they did not call because they were busy at work, they were short of cash, they lost the woman's telephone number, they had not called in a month and thought they had no right to do so, and so forth. Others told our researchers they did not have the same taste as the woman, the woman was too dumb or too smart, they went back to their old girlfriends, or they met someone new.

The variety of reasons men gave for not calling were numerous and did not always make sense, but I think they were all legitimate. Since relationships between men and women are not logical by nature, there is no reason to expect men's reasons for not continuing a relationship to be logical. But if you apply logic to this first step in relationships, men who do not call are only halting relationships they do not think will work before they get started—which is, after all, the best time to take that action.

This getting-to-know-you stage does not necessarily require dating. It can take from two hours to two or three weeks. If a man meets a woman at a party and talks to her for several hours, by the end of that evening they probably know each other fairly well, and the initial stage has already been completed. The person either has or has not lived up to early expectations. If a woman, in a man's opinion, is not as friendly as she looked, or as cheerful as she appeared, or as smart as she seemed, or even as entertaining as he imagined, he is unlikely to pursue the relationship. In most cases, getting to the next stage depends on fulfilling expectations, nothing more.

When the female researchers read the raw data, at first many of them were very annoyed. They argued that some of the reasons men gave for not calling were ridiculous, stupid, and inaccurate. But after they discussed it among themselves for a while, most of the women concluded it was probably better that these men did not call; these relationships were going nowhere. The women also admitted that after the first date, they often refused to go on second and third dates, for reasons that were just as arbitrary.

Stage Three: Needs and Lifestyles

The next stage in dating commonly takes place from the first date to the sixth or seventh. It is during these dates that partners become acquainted with each other's needs, wants, and lifestyles. This, like the first stage in dating, can take place in a very short period or can take weeks or months. The length of time depends on the nature of the dates and the people involved. If, when dating, the parties get to interact significantly, they'll most likely discover each other's needs, wants, and lifestyles quickly.

It is in this stage that a man and a woman determine whether they actually fit. But this does not always come about on the first, second, third, or even fourth or fifth date. In fact, often they have sex before they decide they are incompatible.

A classic example of this was demonstrated in an episode of the TV show *Frasier*. Frasier is chosen to represent his coworkers at the radio station in negotiations with a very tough new female boss. While negotiating, they are both overcome with desire and make wild, passionate love. Throughout the episode Frasier maintains this is probably the wildest, most passionate love affair he's ever had. He keeps repeating that he's fascinated by the woman. At the end of the episode, she is leaving town, and he is seeing her off at the airport. It's obvious they are still attracted to each other and don't want the relationship to end. He tells her he'll visit her, and she responds, "Yes, we can go jogging together." Seeing the startled look on his face, she asks, "By the way, do you jog?" He mutters, "Yes. Once." Frasier, not being the athletic type, suggests instead that they might go antiquing. "For me, *antiquing* isn't a verb," she tells him. Instantly they know their lifestyles and their tastes are so different that they don't have a future together. As they part, he says, "It's a shame," and she answers, "Yes, it is." They had all kinds of passion, but they did not have the other element necessary for a meaningful relationship: common interests.

Separating Attraction from Compatibility

It is almost a universal experience discovering that you and someone to whom you are attracted are not at all compatible. When I was in my twenties, I went to the beach with a friend. As soon as we arrived, we met two young women. It was a Friday night, and we spent until two or three o'clock in the morning together. By the end of the night, we had paired off and agreed to meet for breakfast. The next day we went to the beach, and in the evening we went to a party and had a great time. Sunday morning most of the people at the party met for breakfast and returned to the beach together. It started raining around two o'clock in the afternoon, and we headed back to the city. The young woman I was with was pleasant and clever, and I thoroughly enjoyed her company.

During the drive, my friend suggested that since Monday was a holiday, we all meet in the city and go to Shakespeare in the Park. I was about to second the suggestion when the young woman with whom I had just spent an entire weekend said scornfully, "Shakespeare. I had that crap in high school. I hated it! Romeo and Juliet, yuck!" Then she went on to tell us about some "doofus" who had taken her to an opera in the park. She had left after ten minutes; to her, it sounded like somebody singing Shakespeare. She described her date as one of those jerks who went to upscale singles places on the East Side and overpaid for drinks. She thought he was a dope.

Immediately, I knew we were completely incompatible. Not only did I like Shakespeare and opera, those overpriced East Side singles bars were where I was misspending my youth and having a heck of good time doing it. I dropped her and her girlfriend off an hour later in a very poor neighborhood in Lower Manhattan. I never asked her out again.

This third stage is really another testing stage. If you're not compatible with someone you're dating, there is no way you'll have a meaningful relationship or even much fun. It's better that relationships that don't work at this basic level be ended as quickly and painlessly as possible.

Stage Four: Steady Dating

The fourth stage in relationships is regular dating. This only means that a man and woman get together on a regular basis and go out. Depending on schedules, this could be anything from every day, to twice a week, to several times a month. Only at this point do men even begin to consider having any type of relationship with a woman. Men typically do not think of themselves as being in some sort of dating relationship until after four to six dates. For women, it frequently takes only half as long.

It's very important, therefore, that during these exploratory dates the woman doesn't let on that she considers the relationship anything other than casual dating. Even if she becomes convinced he is the fulfillment of her dream, she can't let on. The primary reason men drop women during the first month or two of dating is that the women come on too strong too soon. Approximately half of the men we talked to broke up with women they were dating because the women started getting serious prematurely.

When a man dates a woman regularly, in his mind it's still casual dating unless some sort of commitment has been made. He usually doesn't commit to monogamous dating until sometime into the relationship. He may date only the one woman for months and yet feel no obligation not to date other women. This stage runs anywhere from three weeks to three months, depending on the nature of the relationship. His thinking is affected by a number of factors, including how often they have dated, how busy their schedules are, and how long and how well they have known each other.

When people have known each other for a long time before dating, the stages usually don't last as long. If the man and woman have been friends for a year or more, they may not have to go through stages one and two and possibly even not through stage three. They probably already know each other's tastes and whether their lifestyles are compatible. If all this is a given, they may go directly to casual dating and move more quickly to the next step. The whole point of casual dating is to give couples the opportunity to know each other more intimately, to allow them to get to know what kind of movies, books, food, and so forth the other person likes. It is a time to fill each other in on all those details that create a lifestyle. Some couples skip this step, but very few.

Fifth Stage:
Romancing the Woman

Most couples, after dating a short time, enter the romantic stage. It is at this time that men are in courtship mode— bringing flowers and chocolates, going to romantic restaurants, holding doors. This is the stage that women like best. It is as close as most women get to meeting their knight in shining armor. Men today are not knights and their armor does not shine, but some polish it just a bit in the early stages of a relationship.

Keep in mind that men are always trying to please the women they like. If you remember that, you should not have any problems with this stage.

Pleasing You Pleases Him

During this stage, it is very important that you let the man please you. One of the discussions we had with groups of men and women centered on how determined men were to please women, particularly during this romantic period. Some women were surprised, even shocked, when they discovered that if they did not let men pamper them, they would turn off many men and displease most others. Men said that *of course* they wanted to please the women they were with; for some, pleasing women is an essential part of the process.

Naturally, to the dismay of women, all this changes too quickly. Depending on the relationship and the man, the romantic stage is short-lived. During this period a woman should sit back and enjoy herself; it is the most productive thing she can do. He will be happy only when he is making her happy.

Despite the fact that most of the women working with me were feminists, they accepted that during this period declaring your independence and telling men you can take care of yourself was not a good idea. After listening to several hundred men talk about breaking off with women because they started taking over the relationship, even the most independent women agreed the smart move is to enjoy life on the pedestal. It's not that difficult, because if you wait until the next stage in the relationship, some men hand the reins over to the women. In the next stage, not only will you be able to take care of yourself, but most men will insist on it.

Stage Six:
Getting Comfortable

Unfortunately for most women, the next stage of most relationships is the comfortable stage: The couple become so used to each other that they stop feeling they have to always be on their best behavior. They start being themselves. Relationships often self-destruct at this point. If your personalities clash now, there is nothing you can or should do to save the relationship.

However, if breakup threatens because the woman is annoyed that the man has stopped being romantic, the relationship may be salvaged. It's understandable that a woman becomes irritated when her boyfriend, who showed up with roses and candy just a few weeks earlier, now sits on her couch, puts his feet up, watches TV, and takes her for granted. But believe it or not, research shows that taking each other for granted is an important stage in all relationships, and becoming comfortable with the other person is a hallmark of almost all serious relationships. The prudent woman thus will not think of it as a deal killer.

Still, I don't recommend that women stop complaining about being taken for granted. If you let yourself be taken for granted without protest, it dramatically increases the likelihood that the relationship will not go anywhere. This is one of the first red flags. When a relationship that seemed to be going along beautifully begins to run into one stumbling block after another, it is often because the man has begun to lose respect for the woman. He no longer treats her as if she's special. In the worst case, she becomes a doormat. The message she sends is that she is there for his convenience.

An interesting part of this phenomenon is that the woman, in an attempt to correct the situation, sometimes starts knocking herself out to do everything for the man—washing his underwear, cleaning his house, and so on. This, interestingly enough, does not endear the woman to him or improve the situation. It simply reinforces the notion that the woman is there for his convenience.

Domestic Discord

Women at one time gained respect from men by withholding sex.

Today, women who withhold doing household chores usu-
ally get more respect from men than those who don't.

Nearly 17 percent of the women coming out of marriage license bureaus who had their own places said they knew how to cook but had never, or only on special occasions, cooked for the man they were about to marry. They reasoned they were likely to be cooking for fifty years once they were married, and they preferred to delay the inevitable.

More than three hundred women we interviewed coming out of marriage license bureaus refused to clean their man's home—or do anything of a similar nature—on the premise that it wasn't their job. They explained politely to their fiancés that they were not going to undertake those tasks. Their future husbands accepted their decisions, and more than half said they respected the women for standing up for themselves. (If you are already doing these things for a man, however, it is not smart to quit suddenly without explanation; instead, taper off slowly until you're back to doing chores only on special occasions.)

We also spoke to hundreds of women coming out of marriage license bureaus who had cleaned and cooked for their fiancés on a regular basis. Most of them said their men were very good to them, and they were just responding in kind. The men in these relationships were usually very helpful. I suspect it wasn't an even division of labor, but these men did help with the dishes, change the oil in the woman's car, help her move, and so forth. Being a loving, helpful partner is fine, it seems, but being a servant is not.

The comfortable stage usually has several hallmarks. One,

the man does not have to call for a date, and may not feel obliged to call before he drops in. He is as welcome in your house as he is in his own. You expect to see him often, and you do. This can be a positive sign. The more time a man spends with a woman—the more he takes her for granted, ironically—the more serious he is likely to become. If he comes over every evening, gets a Coke, puts his feet up, and settles in to watch television, even if it seems unromantic, it may be a sign of commitment. The men we questioned told us it was at that point they first considered the women theirs. This mutual sense of ownership is the next step in commitment. It indicates that, in the man's mind, you and he are connected in a special way.

The comfortable stage usually sets in after three months. A woman should look on it as an announcement that the man considers this a potentially serious relationship. You must find out, because if he is not starting to commit to the relationship at this point, it's likely to go nowhere. In the early stages of becoming comfortable, you must also become a couple, which means the relationship is monogamous. Only after this do most men start to think about marriage.

There's a second reason women should insist on the relationship becoming monogamous early in the comfortable stage: Only after a relationship has been monogamous for a few months can you safely introduce the subject of marriage. But don't start pushing for a proposal yet. At this time, you aren't seeking commitment, only information.

Respect Yourself

In addition to interviewing engaged couples, we conducted a focus group with men who broke up with women while in the comfortable stage. They usually broke up within a month of entering this stage. Almost invariably, the woman had made her life secondary to his, and he lost respect for her. The women who insisted on being treated well, on going out occasionally and being taken to nice restaurants, and on his dressing up on occasion were almost twice as likely to end up marrying the man as those who did not. Those who let men walk all over them ended up almost as servants. As one insightful man put it, "No one marries a servant."

Boys on the Town

There is a second problem that often occurs in this stage, and that is "boys' night out." If a man has become comfortable with you, he should be monogamous. If he doesn't become monogamous at almost the same time he becomes comfortable, you may have a major problem. If he openly says he is occasionally going out with someone else, you need to reconsider your options. If he's going out with other women, he is most likely not thinking of you as a potential mate. Most men, however, are not that open about having other relationships, so you need to pay attention.

You can't expect the man in your life to give up going to football games with his buddies the minute he meets you. Nor should he give up going out with the boys after he's married. He'll still want to go to sporting events and do other things with his pals. He'll probably want to do those things even though many of his friends are still single. But there's a built-in problem: If he continues to go out regularly, especially on weekends, with his single friends, he is likely to meet other women. I don't care what he is doing, unless he goes directly to a sporting event and comes home right after it ends, there is a very good possibility that a group of single men are going to look for women. Not every man who goes out on a weekend with the boys is going to chase women, of course. But once he becomes part of a couple, he should not be going out regularly with single men and to singles places. If he continues to do so, the chances that the relationship will develop into marriage are slim.

We questioned men who had broken up with women after reaching this stage in a relationship. Twenty-nine percent of them said they had met someone else. Half of them said they met the other woman during their daily routine—commuting, business travel, at work. The other half said they met the other woman when they were out with their single pals.

Two men gave a detailed account of when, where, and why they had cheated on their steady girlfriends. When we asked them whether, when they were dating one woman, they had cheated on her, one answered, "I guess, sort of," and the other said, "A couple of times." We asked how it happened. Both said they were in a singles place with a single friend who wanted to pick up a woman. The woman had someone with her, and they ended up with the second woman. Their story was repeated over and over by the men we questioned who went to singles bars.

One of the things you must insist on if you want your relationship to last is monogamy—which means you should insist that your boyfriend stop going to singles places. Even if your man doesn't cheat, the chances that your relationship will lead to marriage are nearly cut in half if he does not take seriously the monogamous nature of your relationship and refuses to stop living like a single guy.

Stage Seven:
Committed Couplehood

The most important stage in any relationship is becoming a couple, because once you become a couple, both parties make major commitments. People who become couples frequently end up marrying. I have interviewed people who have been going together for as long as ten years and never became a couple. Steady dating does not necessarily imply commitment.

There are three characteristics that all successful couples share. First, they are monogamous; they date each other and no one else. What's more, they don't do things that would make it seem they might be less than monogamous. They don't go away for weekends with the boys or with the girls, and they don't hang out in singles places.

You're Number One

The second characteristic of a successful couple is that both people put their partner's interests above their friends and family—not that they break off relations, but that they make their partners their first priority. There are, of course, times when one will go to a family function the other doesn't think is important, or will spend some time with friends when the partner would rather they didn't.

Unless a man regularly puts the needs and desires of his friends and family above those of his partner, a woman should not get upset and endanger their relationship. Many women coming out of marriage license bureaus said they respected or even admired the close relationship their fiancés had with their families. Some believed that watching the way a man treats his family and his friends gives you an insight into his operative values. Almost one-third of the women judged their fiancés by how they treated their families. They believed it was a good predictor of how the men would eventually treat their wives and children. Almost half the women we questioned said they thought there was some truth in this but they were not sure how much, while approximately 20 percent thought it was nonsense.

You must keep in mind that the strength of family obligations will vary from one family to another. There are some families with very strong ties, relationships, and duties. If he comes from one of those families, even after you become the primary person in his life, he will also feel a strong obligation to members of his family, whether immediate or extended. You have to respect those relationships. If you are not the primary interest in his life, however, it is very serious problem. To be his primary interest does not mean that every time there's a conflict between you and his family he'll put your interests first, but rather that most of the time he will consider your needs and desires before he considers his family's.

Stand By Your Woman

One of the most important indicators of the depth of a man's commitment is his willingness to protect his partner from attacks by his family. Coming out of marriage license bureaus, a number of men told our researchers that their mother, sisters, or someone else in the family did not like their bride-to-be. If the family member says something in private, most men will come to their woman's defense. But when a member of his family says something critical to or about his fiancée in public, a man is obliged to defend her. Seventy-nine percent of these men said that when a family member made a negative comment about their fiancée, they came to her defense.

Take Karl, a second-generation American. Both his mother and his father and all his mother's brothers and sisters had come from East Germany thirty years ago when it was still a communist regime, divided from West Germany. Being strangers in this country, family became very important to them. Every Sunday afternoon, they gathered for a meal at his mother's house. Karl's aunts, his brother's wife, and his two sisters each brought parts of the meal. After eating, they spent the afternoon together as a family, talking, watching TV, or playing pinochle. When Karl started showing up with Sheila, it announced to everyone there that she was a potential family member. It was obvious to his family that he was serious about her. He had never before brought a woman to these family gatherings.

His mother expressed her dislike of Sheila because she was not of German descent. Two weeks after Karl defended Sheila to his family, his mother announced that the family dinners were now going to be held on Saturday afternoons. She knew Sheila had to work on Saturdays. The following Saturday Karl visited his family in the morning but did not stay for dinner. When his mother called to ask where he was, he said he would have been there if it was on Sunday. Sheila could not be there, therefore he was not coming. Karl did not show up for the next three weeks. His mother switched the family gatherings back to Sundays (which made everyone happy, because they did not like having dinner on Saturdays).

Karl stood by the woman he planned to marry. He let his

mother know that Sheila was important in his life and that there was nothing she could do to change that.

We heard a number of similar stories, and they all came down to the same thing: Family members did not like the woman the man had chosen, and they let him know about it. He in turn let them know in no uncertain terms that he was not going to let their feelings interfere with the relationship. If your relationship is in this stage, but he does not defend you, your relationship could be in grave danger.

Hanging Out

The third essential characteristic of successful couples is they hang out together. When they are doing nothing and have nothing to do, they do it together. This is a very critical stage, yet a lot of people don't recognize it. Unless a couple enjoys each other's company so much that they don't need a special activity, a dinner, a play, or a movie to have fun, they have a problem.

When just being together is enough, you are a successful couple.

Stage Eight: Premarital Couplehood

Successful couples do not always marry. Sometimes they get along so well they live happily together for years, and for some reason the man never commits. Committed couples have three characteristics. First, they're affectionate. It is not that they hug and kiss all the time, although they often show signs of physical affection. They touch each other, hold hands, and are openly affectionate.

This affection is common among couples who are headed for the altar. While affectionate behavior is a hallmark of commitment, it often occurs earlier in a relationship.

It is usually only committed couples, however, who sacrifice for each other. Both parties constantly do small things to please their partners. Women go to war movies because they know the man in their life wants to see shoot-'em-ups. Men sit through chick flicks such as *Sleepless in Seattle* even though they would rather be in a dentist's chair.

Most men in love are constantly doing things to please their partner. If your partner goes out of his way to please you all the time, you've reached the point that a marriage proposal should be expected. If you let this time go by, you are making a very serious mistake. Timing is critical. We'll explore in the next chapter how to best handle this situation.

Closely Held Secrets

Another hallmark of premarital couples is they become confidants. They feel free to say anything to each other. She will tell him that she doesn't like his brother, his sister's boyfriend, his best friends, or his mother's cooking, knowing that her comments will never get back to his brother, sister, friends, or mother. He likewise will tell her what he thinks about most things. When they discuss anything, there is an unwritten agreement that their comments will never go beyond the two of them. It is probably the most sacred covenant unmarried couples have. If one of them betrays this covenant, it's an indication that they are not as close as they should be.

If you are not confidants in this stage, it raises a red flag, because more than 90 percent of couples on the road to marriage are.

Two words of warning: First, we ran across fifteen couples who broke up because the man objected to his girlfriend's comments about his family. Do not think because your boyfriend or fiancé does not react emotionally to your comments that you haven't struck a nerve (see the second warning below), or that because he keeps your confidence, he doesn't object to what you've said. Men love their families as much as women and are usually sensitive to any criticism of family members. I used comments about the man's family to demonstrate the importance of keeping confidences, not to imply it is safe for a woman to make such comments.

Second, men don't share their feelings easily, and it's unreasonable to expect them to do so. Most men will tell you what they think, not what they feel—sometimes even after many years of marriage.

Timing Matters

The timing of these stages is important, but there is no schedule carved in stone. Unusual circumstances can change the timing of relationships. If one or both of you work crazy hours or you live a distance apart, either factor could slow down the process. You would be very foolish to end a promising relationship because the man you're seeing is a few days or weeks behind schedule. You may wish to reexamine your options, however, if he is months or years behind schedule.

If after three or four dates he isn't calling you regularly, or—even worse—if he only calls sporadically, the chances the relationship will lead to marriage are slight. If after seven or ten dates he's not calling regularly, it's probably wise to look elsewhere.

You should go from casual dating to monogamous dating

in anywhere from one to four months. If you're behind schedule becoming monogamous, unless there are unusual circumstances, you may have a problem. The fact that you go places together, do things together, and all your friends think you are a couple is not meaningful. You're a couple only when you're monogamous. Most couples reach this point in three to four months. If your relationship isn't monogamous by six months, there is a real possibility that it's never going to be.

The freedom and security to share confidences should develop shortly after you become monogamous. If they haven't, it could be a sign your relationship isn't progressing as it should.

It usually takes between six months and a year before a couple becomes committed, although there are exceptions. Remember, one of the steps in a developing relationship for men is putting their partner's interests above those of their friends and family. Our surveys found it takes most couples nearly a year to reach this stage. If after a year this has not occurred, your relationship lacks commitment. Seventy-three percent of people coming out of marriage license bureaus said that within nine months, their partner had become the center of their lives. Only 7 percent reported that it took them more than a year to become a committed couple.

Love Potion Number Nine: The Proposal Stage

I put the proposal stage at the end of the timing section because in this stage timing is critical. If at the end of twenty-two months a man has not proposed, the chances that he will propose start to diminish. As the twenty-second month approaches, you should do whatever you can to get him to commit. It is not that after twenty-two months the chances a man will propose evaporate—they do not. But it's a watershed moment, when the statistical trend line begins to drop off.

Most men propose after going with a woman for eighteen months. If you haven't received a proposal by then, it's time to start dropping very broad hints. Don't bother with subtle hints—men simply don't pick them up. You should try to get him to commit in the next four to six months. This is the high-commitment period for most men in serious relationships. For the next three and a half years, the likelihood of a proposal diminishes gradually; after that, it begins to plunge dramatically. If you've been with a man for four, five, or six years, you may still get a proposal—but once the relationship has passed the seven-year mark, the prospects are almost nil.

A Word of Advice

Don't be ruled by the nine stages outlined in this chapter—they are estimates based on statistical averages. No two relationships develop in exactly the same way or at the same rate. In many successful relationships, the stages overlap and/or fall into different patterns. One in five couples we spoke to coming out of a marriage license bureau skipped at least one step. We met five couples who had known each other less than two weeks before becoming engaged. Obviously, they fast-forwarded through most of the stages.

Nevertheless, understanding the stages of a relationship is worthwhile. It gives you insight into how successful relationships are formed and some idea of what to expect. This study of the nature of relationships is not designed to be used as a set of hard-and-fast criteria to measure the success or soundness of your relationship; nor should it be used as an excuse to end a relationship if there is still a good chance of success. This chapter was designed to give you a diagnostic tool you can use to examine your relationship and work at improving it.

Relationship Recap, Statistically Speaking:

➤ Don't get tied up in knots and start doubting yourself if a man doesn't call. It's probably because you did not live up to his inaccurate, unrealistic expectations.

➤ If you want to impress a man, early in the relationship show concern for his future, his health, or his career.

➤ Never speak of marriage, children, or your future together during the first half a dozen dates.

➤ If you and he have nothing in common except animal attraction, the relationship will not work in the long term.

➤ Men think of regular dating as casual dating, whereas women often assume they are already a couple.

➤ When a man wants to be romantic, enjoy it while you can. Courtship gives a man a chance to please his woman. Let him.

➤ When he gets so comfortable he takes you for granted, you should speak out, but you should also understand that it is part of most serious relationships.

➤ Before marriage, refrain from waiting on your man and doing his household chores. Allow him to pamper you.

➤ Couples on the road to marriage should be and usually are monogamous within six months.

➤ When hanging out together is enough, you are a successful couple.

➤ If you regularly make small sacrifices for each other and share confidences, and if you have dated exclusively for a year, the next step ought to be a proposal.

➤ This chapter was designed to help save and assess relationships—not scuttle them.

5

Speaking of Marriage

I F YOU WANT to discuss marriage with the man in your life, you are probably going to have to broach the subject first.

When we asked couples about to marry which of them had first spoken about marriage, 69 percent said it was the woman, 12 percent the man. The remainder did not remember, were not sure, or disagreed. Most of the times they disagreed, the man said it was the woman, and she did not remember it that way.

When it came to who had proposed marriage, only 4 percent said it was the woman. However, after questioning the men and women separately and then as couples, we came to the conclusion a figure of 9 percent more accurately reflects what actually took place. Less than 2 percent of the engaged women took on the traditional male role and asked, "Will you marry me?" or its equivalent. The remaining 7 percent asked without an actual *Will you marry me* or similar phrase. Most of the women whom we concluded had proposed denied proposing—and they had a legitimate point. In more than half the cases where a woman proposed and the man virtually accepted, the man proposed as well.

Mary and Robert are a typical example of the role reversal. Robert complained that after she proposed and he accepted, she made him get down on one knee and ask her to marry him. She told him if he didn't, she would walk out the door.

Without any doubt, men still traditionally pop the question. So when I suggest that you talk to your man about marriage, I don't necessarily mean propose—but bring the subject up.

But I Thought You Knew

Discussing marriage is important for a number of reasons. One of the most important is to avoid a misunderstanding that can strike a major blow to your plans to marry. I interviewed dozens of women who, after years in a relationship, broached the subject of marriage, only to be told by their lover that he had never had any intention of marrying them or anyone else. The women who received that response all asked the same question: "Why didn't you tell me earlier?" And the men all gave the same answer: "You never asked."

If you don't know what your man thinks about marriage, you'll have to bring up the subject and listen carefully to what he says. If he tries to avoid the topic or talk around it, don't let him. You must find out what he thinks about marrying in general, but more importantly, what he thinks about the possibility of marrying you.

Celeste is the classic example of why you must know. She met Mark, an attorney, at a party and went out with him half a dozen times but never slept with him. On their seventh date he told her he and four of his male friends were going on a cruise in two weeks. Two of the friends were going alone, and two were taking their girlfriends. Mark explained to Celeste that he would like to take her, but the other two couples would be sharing a bed, and since they had not yet been intimate, he didn't know what to do. Mark assured her that if she went, neither of them should consider it a commitment, and their lives would go on as usual. Celeste slept with him on their next date and went on the cruise. More than a year later, when Celeste told him that someday she intended to marry and have children, Mark told her she had better find another guy, reminding her that they had a "no-strings" agreement—in his mind, the discussion they'd had about commitment more than a year earlier still applied!

Believe it or not, three other women told very similar stories. If you and your man have ever talked about having a relationship without commitment, you had better clarify your position.

Not talking about marriage is a problem for another reason. Our female researchers were shocked to find that men were reluctant to bring up the subject of marriage even after they had been thinking favorably about it for months. We talked to dozens of men who had been in serious relationships. At least at one point in those relationships, they had thought seriously about marriage, but they had never told the woman what they were thinking. The relationship ended without either party bringing up the subject.

Insist on Marriage

Our most important discovery was that the primary difference between women who marry and women who do not is:

Women who marry insist that the men in their lives marry them.

I know that seems like an oversimplification, but it is an undeniable statistical fact, and it's crucial. More than 73 percent of the women coming out of marriage license bureaus with their future husbands told us they had put pressure on their man to get a proposal. In most cases, this pressure didn't involve an attempt to manipulate their man into marrying them but was simply a result of their telling their man what they were feeling.

In a variety of ways, the women let their men know they did not think they could live happy or fulfilled lives unless they were married. The idea that any woman needs a man to be happy and fulfilled today seems politically incorrect. Nevertheless, 64 percent of the brides-to-be told us they held this belief, while less than 20 percent of the women who did not think they would marry held the same belief.

These statistics came from two surveys. For the first, we polled women coming out of marriage license bureaus, and for the second we polled women in their late thirties or forties who thought it was unlikely they would marry. I was not convinced by those surveys indicating that a woman who believed she needed a man to be happy was more likely to find one. I thought it was not only possible but probable that these women were giving the only answers that women in their positions could give. Naturally, a woman who is about to marry would like to believe that marriage is necessary for her happiness and, therefore, is more likely to say marriage is necessary. On the other hand, women who believe they are not going to marry, for their own well-being, must convince themselves that they can live happy, fulfilled lives without a man.

The numbers were so striking, however, that I set up a separate study to test the thesis. We identified 148 women between the ages of twenty-three and twenty-eight who said they wanted to marry but were not presently in a relationship likely to lead to marriage. We asked these single women if they thought marriage was necessary for them to have a happy, complete, and fulfilled life. Next, we arranged to interview them again after four years. After the agreed-upon time, it was possible to interview only 102 of them. We suspect they were difficult to contact because many of them had married and changed their names, but since we couldn't confirm that this was the case, we did not factor these women into the study. Among those we were able to reach, we found that those who had told our researchers four years earlier that marriage was essential to their happiness were almost twice as likely to be engaged or married as those who said they thought marriage was not essential to their happiness. I was not surprised by these numbers; nor were my female researchers. We concluded that a woman who believed that marriage was essential to her happiness worked harder at finding a mate.

Powerful Beliefs

We ran two focus groups at the end of the follow-up interviews with women who thought that marriage was essential to their happiness and women who did not. In addition, we compared women coming out of marriage license bureaus with women in their late thirties and forties who were not married or in a serious relationship.

After reviewing the data, we came to this conclusion: If the woman conveyed to the man in her life the belief that marriage was essential to her happiness, it often became a very powerful argument for marriage. Almost a third of the women who were about to marry said that the discussion or argument that convinced their fiancé to propose went something like this: "Marriage is essential to my happiness. If you love me as you claim, you'll do what it takes to make me happy."

While only a handful of men said they were convinced by this argument alone, many indicated that it was very powerful and did play a major part in their decision to propose. In fact, several pointed out that once a woman made that argument, if you loved her, you had no choice—what else could you do?

Not all men, or even the majority, said or implied they were trapped into marrying. Approximately one-third told us the only reason they proposed to the woman was that they were in love with her and wanted to spend the rest of their life with her. The main pressure felt by these grooms was a product of their uncertainty about the answer they would receive when they proposed. These fellows were dubbed the "Prince Charmings" by the female researchers.

Men coming out of the marriage license bureaus usually did not fall into neat categories. They were neither poor slobs who were bulldozed or tricked into marrying, nor Prince Charmings who could not live another moment without the woman of their dreams. While most admitted they felt some pressure to propose, the men said their primary reason for proposing was that they were in love. What's more:

A majority were adamant in their belief that pressure merely sped up the process—it was not the deciding factor.

These men said that their brides-to-be were in a greater hurry to get hitched than they were, but they figured the trip to the altar was inevitable.

We asked the men this: "If the pressure had been removed and you had felt free to propose on your own schedule, when would you have proposed?" Interestingly, 63 percent said they would have proposed in a year or two. That's a very revealing answer: Our research showed that when men delayed proposing by as little as three months, often they never proposed. So this pressure that seemed to be relevant only in terms of timing may have had a great deal more significance than the respondents believed—without such pressure, there probably wouldn't have been a proposal at all!

While men are very hesitant to admit they do anything under pressure, they did concede in focus groups that being put under pressure motivated them to propose. When we asked these men what they thought would have happened if they had postponed making a proposal for as little as three to four months, 50 percent said their future brides would have been upset. They explained that their women were expecting a proposal. In approximately 90 percent of the cases, the women had conveyed to the men that they expected a proposal without ever saying so openly. When we asked the future grooms at what point they knew or felt their partner expected them to eventually propose, most told us it was very early in the relationship. We then wanted to know if they had felt pressured as soon as they received the message. To our surprise, 71 percent said no. The message was nonthreatening because it was not *Someday we will marry,* but *If we take this relationship to the point where marriage becomes the next step, I'm the marrying kind, and I'll expect a proposal.*

The women agreed that they had let the men know early in the relationship that they were going to marry someday. The majority of those women also believed that their men understood if they remained a couple for a year or more and were getting along, at that point they should start seriously considering marriage. This is an extremely good idea: Left to their own devices, less than 7 percent of their future husbands thought dating for a year and being in love meant marriage was necessarily the next step.

Broad Hints

The women who understood that the man in their life needed a little push in the right direction, but dropped very subtle hints, were rarely successful. Most women we interviewed believed that since they had been hinting they wanted to marry for months, the men in their lives had gotten the message. Several told us they thought that because their boyfriends were articulate, well educated, and sophisticated, they would pick up subtle hints, but interviews with the men showed this was often not so. Vague hints or subtle messages aimed at men very seldom work. If you want a man to act, while it is not wise to come right out and tell him bluntly, your hints must be broad and your message delivered with the subtlety of a sledgehammer. It's the difference between saying "I see us married someday" and "I see us married by next year."

"Next year" frames the statement more concretely, which is what men need.

When we asked the grooms how their brides let them know that they expected a ring, only 5 percent said their fiancées came right out and told them. The rest said, "Women let you know things by hinting." When we asked the brides how they let the grooms know they expected a marriage proposal sooner or later, most said they told them what they expected. Sixty-three percent of the engaged women explained to us that at least once, they had told the man in their life that they expected their relationship to lead to marriage. What the men heard was that the women expected their relationship to eventually lead to marriage—someday. They felt no sense of urgency, nor did they even think of time as important. More than one-third of the brides-to-be reported that months after they were certain that their boyfriends realized they expected a marriage proposal, something their boyfriends said or did let them know that marriage was the farthest thing from their thoughts. When they made this discovery, they became more direct in their approach.

"It's Time"

This brings us to the message most brides sent to their future husbands: *It's time to get married.* The women we interviewed said they got this idea across in a number of ways: "All my friends are getting married." "My biological clock is ticking." "I think if we got married, we'd be able to save some money." "Everybody wants to know when we're going to take the plunge."

After a woman knows, not guesses, that the man in her life

is favorably disposed to the idea of marriage, she should send a *Let's-do-it-now* message. Without it, her man may put off proposing until he no longer thinks it important or necessary.

Some kinds of pressure seem to produce positive results, while other types very seldom work. While a number of grooms told us pressure to propose came from the bride's family, this does not usually produce the desired effect. We interviewed a number of men who broke off relationships because they could not stand the pressure from the bride's family.

A substantial percentage of men said they felt uncomfortable every time they met the bride's family and resented the family putting pressure on them. Many men said that only the woman they were dating had the right to even bring up the subject of marriage. The reality is that most men are feeling some pressure when they propose, but it's usually pressure from the woman, not her family.

The exception to that rule appeared when the bride's family announced that the bride, in effect, had a dowry: "When you marry our daughter, we will buy your first house," or "We'll take you into the family business," or some other financial incentive.

When we questioned women who were about to be married, they did not for a second deny they had put pressure on their men. In fact, 72 percent of them said they had coaxed, seduced, talked, pushed, directed, and nudged their future husbands into proposing. The vast majority thought the man in their life was ready to propose, and they were just facilitating the process. Fewer than 15 percent of the women realized that if they hadn't pushed for a proposal, it would probably never have come. Those who did understand that time was a critical factor relied on their instincts or intuition.

Strike While the Groom Is Hot

The women were not able to give reasons for their conviction that their man was ready to propose, but it was compelling enough for them to act on. They took every imaginable step, from hinting to whining, begging, and bullying, to get the man to propose immediately. When we asked why, one woman in a focus group put it colorfully: "You have to strike while the groom is hot." A majority of the engaged women agreed that while they had not pushed for an immediate proposal, most of them had a sense that the time was ripe.

Our next study dealt with the reaction of men when marriage was brought up for the first time. The only men we used for this study were of prime marriageable age (see chapter 1). This isn't the legal age at which a man can marry, of course, but the age when men are ready to marry. We made sure the men were out of school long enough and had an adequate income or were established in their careers.

Gut Reactions

The bad news is that when marriage is seriously discussed for the first time, most men's reaction is clearly negative. The good news is that one-third of the men we talked to, after seriously discussing marriage, decided to get married. Most did not immediately propose, but after getting used to the idea, they accepted or even celebrated the idea of marrying. If they thought they had reasons not to get married, these were usually very practical ones—finishing school, getting a new job, earning enough money, or even getting out of an apartment lease to find a new place where the two of them could live. They most often told the woman they wanted to marry her within a week or two of the first discussion. There was nothing vague about their intentions. Although they seldom set a date, they were clear they planned to marry in the immediate future.

Many of the couples we spoke to who fell into this category said there was no formal proposal of marriage. They knew they were going to get married long before they went out and bought a ring. In this group, about one-third of the women went with the man to buy the ring. These were people who had a relaxed, informal relationship, and it carried over into how they handled this situation. When we asked if the man proposed after he bought the ring, one woman said: "Why should he get down on one knee after we bought the ring together? I wasn't going to give him that much time. When the jeweler handed him the ring over the counter, he just slipped it on my finger. That's what I wanted and expected."

Some of the men who immediately accepted the idea of getting married were very romantic; they bought champagne or proposed on Valentine's Day or Christmas. The couples who agreed right away to marry were not unrealistic romantics with their heads in the clouds. They most often followed their agreement to marry with very serious discussions about various aspects of marriage that were designed to head off problems before they occurred. If they had religious differences, they discussed in which religion they would raise the children. Sometimes they discussed money—who owed what and how they would share the expenses. They also discussed where they would live, where their kids would go to school, and whose job requirements would take precedence. They tried to smooth out as many of the bumps as they could before they got on the road to marriage.

Most discussions after a couple have mutually agreed to spend their lives together are honest and straightforward and cover a variety of topics. Occasionally, though, these discussions end the relationship. This is most likely when the couple had postponed discussing basic beliefs, religion, or money during their courtship.

One of the great myths is that marriages are always dashed on romantic rocks. More often, marriage proposals founder on life's practical rocks. When we spoke to newlyweds and couples at marriage license bureaus, we discovered that a number of them had been in serious relationships before the one that led to marriage. In many cases, those relationships had fallen apart because of differences about religion, politics, families not getting along, and so forth. The reasons for people breaking up were numerous, but most were good ones. The researchers and I agreed that the couples who called off marriage at this point were very sensible, levelheaded people; if they had married, the marriages would probably have broken up for the same reasons the couples broke up before marriage. Theirs was a far less complicated, expensive, and painful solution.

Many of the women in this group loved the idea of getting the ring and being proposed to, but from what we saw of their discussions, a proposal was often an afterthought. They were like business executives who make a deal and shake hands on it, then get together a couple of days later to sign the contract. These couples reported that they often moved from a discussion of marriage to planning a wedding without realizing when the exact transition took place. As far as they were concerned, it was a natural development.

Initial Reactions

When the young woman brings up the subject of marriage and the man either instantly or within a short period of time accepts the idea that they are going to marry, a woman has a seemingly simple path to follow. All she has to do is plan the wedding. But since two-thirds of men react with some trepidation (if not negatively) to the idea of getting married, how a woman handles her man's initial reaction to the idea is critical to getting him to the altar. Keep in mind that of the men we spoke to coming out of marriage license bureaus, two-thirds had an initial reaction not of "Yes, let's do it" but "No, let's not" or at least "Not now."

Hundreds of women told us they interpreted any response other than "Yes, dear" as a rejection—which is unfortunate, because in many cases it wasn't a rejection so much as a reaction to a subject with which most men are uncomfortable. In fact, how a woman handles this reaction, which may strike her as bizarre, often influences the future of the relationship. It can and sometimes does determine whether the man ends the relationship or proposes marriage.

The answer that most enrages women—and an answer often given by men—is, "I really haven't seriously thought about marriage" or something similar. The vast majority of the women who asked their men what they thought of marriage and received this answer said they were surprised, shocked, outraged, astounded, and even angry. Many of them read that answer as: *I don't love you; I don't want any part of you; I don't want to marry you or anyone else; I'm out of here.* More than a hundred women coming out of marriage license bureaus told us they'd had previous serious relationships that they'd ended because the man told them he had never thought seriously about marriage. Their reaction was not unique. We also interviewed a number of women in their late thirties and forties who were in serious relationships when the man gave them the "I haven't really thought about marriage" answer, and they broke off the relationship. A very dumb thing to do.

While some men used the "I haven't thought about it" response to let a woman know he had no intention of pursuing the relationship, much less marrying her, this is often not what the answer means. In the vast majority of cases, the man is telling the truth. I know that's almost impossible for most women to believe, because many of them have been thinking about marriage since they were little girls. A number of our interviewees said they had been planning their wedding since they were nine years old. When we interviewed the men coming out of marriage license bureaus who'd told their fiancées they hadn't thought about getting married, one-third didn't remember saying it. The other two-thirds remembered, but most of them didn't give it much significance. When we told them it upset their brides, a typical response was, "That wasn't my intention. What did she want me to do, lie to her?"

More than 90 percent of the men didn't think the answer was a rejection; it was simply a fact. When we spoke to the women, most of them were still convinced it was a "no" answer. When I explained to them that it was not, many were incredulous. They asked, "How could he not know? I've been hinting about it for months." Or, "Come on, he can't be that dense."

If the man in your life lives by himself or with other men or hangs out with other men, I can assure you the subject of marriage almost never comes up. And if it is discussed, it's discussed in a macho, jovial way: "Who, me, need a ball and chain?" It's not a subject men talk glowingly about or about at all. Even if the man you're going out with lives at home with his mother and his father, unless he has sisters of marriageable age, the subject has probably not been discussed much. If it's brought up in conversation, most often it's between his sisters and their mother, and usually when the young man is not present.

The best response for any woman who gets that kind of answer from a man is, "Maybe it's time for you to think about it." It's also about time for her to make her hints a lot less subtle. Men are not subtle creatures, and I have to keep reminding women that they can't expect men to think the way they think. Men are not from Mars, nor are women from Venus. The sexes are much farther apart than that.

You may wonder why saying something as simple as "Maybe it's time for you to think about it" is necessary. When we talked to the men outside marriage license bureaus, we found that within four months of giving the "haven't thought about it" answer to a woman, a substantial percentage proposed. Statistically, in fact, it is one of the most encouraging answers a woman can receive.

Take Tom, for example. It didn't occur to him that his offhand remark—"I've never thought seriously about getting married"—would hurt the woman he loved. He had been going with Beth for almost a year and a half when they went to a movie. Just before the movie started, Beth leaned over and asked him if he'd ever thought about the two of them getting married. As he was telling her he hadn't, the lights started to fade and the movie trailers started.

His version of the next few minutes was dramatically different than hers. According to him, after she asked the question and the lights dimmed, he started thinking about it. In less than five minutes he decided it was a great idea and leaned over and said, "Let's do it. Let's get married." Tom added that when she turned so he could see her face, he saw she was crying. When we asked why he thought she was crying, he said, "Oh, you know women. I gave her a hug and kiss and went back to watching the movie."

Beth's account was quite different. The minute he said he hadn't thought about marrying her, she started crying. She felt rejected. She was on the verge of walking out when he leaned over and said, "Let's do it." When we told her about his comments she said, "Tom's a good guy and I love him—but he can be really dense."

What "Not Ready" Means

The second most common answer that women read as negative is, "I'm not ready yet." If a man is of a marriageable age, it may be just that—he's simply not ready. If a man has been out of school long enough, is employed, and is earning enough to support a family, that answer isn't a good sign; there's a good chance that "I'm not ready" means no. But there's about an equal chance that it's nothing more than a stress reaction. The first thing any woman should ask is, "Why aren't you ready?" That's a very sensible question, and sometimes the answer will clarify his position.

A number of women had fiancés who said they weren't ready when the subject of marriage was first broached. Most of these women asked why, and in many cases the problem solved itself. One young woman we interviewed asked the man she had been dating for almost a year why he wasn't ready. He told her he didn't think it would be fair to burden her with his college debt. He still owed seventeen thousand dollars to Uncle Sam.

He was planning to ask her to marry him three months after he made the last payment. He figured it would take him that long to save enough to purchase a ring. When she asked him how long it would take, he gave her an exact date. He had obviously thought about it. He figured at five hundred dollars a month it would take thirty-four months to pay off his loan and buy the ring. He was delighted when she told him she didn't want to wait almost three years and would be happy to help him pay his college debt. This conversation took place six weeks before we met them outside a marriage license bureau.

The answers that women received when they asked why their boyfriends were not ready to marry ran the gamut from mundane to astounding. One man in New York City said he had a year earlier signed a three-year lease on a tiny one-bedroom apartment. He was convinced they couldn't both live there, but he was stuck with the lease and couldn't afford a second apartment. Worse, his lease didn't permit subletting. He had even talked to a lawyer about the possibility of breaking the lease, but the lawyer was dubious. When he told her what the problem was, she moved in with him the next week, and the following month I met them at a marriage license bureau.

Some men do present insurmountable problems. When Julie told me about her previous boyfriend, Ed, I found her story so fantastic I asked if I could contact him. He confirmed the tale. When Julie asked Ed why she would have to wait for him to propose, he very calmly explained that he couldn't do it until his mother died. His mother, Edna, could not get around easily, he said, and he had to do her shopping. Ed insisted he had to live with his mother because she often needed something in the middle of the night, and if he lived elsewhere, he'd be driving over several nights a week. This tale upset Julie; she had attended Edna's sixty-third birthday party a few months earlier, and Edna seemed to be in excellent health. In an effort to calm Julie down, Ed said he would marry her if she would move in with his mother. He cautioned, however, that he was not making a firm offer. He would first have to get his mother's permission to marry and then ask her if they could live in her house.

In our conversation, Ed told us he was glad Julie had said no. Ed didn't think Julie would have gotten along with his mother—or his grandmother, who also lived at the house.

Most men are more reasonable. When they say they are not ready, it's because they don't have enough money. When we talked to men at marriage license bureaus who had at some point given their future bride this answer, they said that getting married sooner would have created a financial hardship. The men almost unanimously noted that when they got married, they became responsible for the support of their wives and any future children. And no matter how the laws have changed to balance out gender inequities, traditionally judges rule in divorces that men are responsible for financial support.

Most men believe that when a woman marries, she is not making the same type of commitment a man does. Most women disagree, some vehemently. Nevertheless, the fact is that this is what most men believe, and there is no point in debating them, because men's actions or lack of action in most situations are dictated by how they see the world. Men who think this way genuinely believe "I'm not ready yet" is the only responsible answer they can give. In many cases, it's an indication that the man is an earnest person, so you shouldn't automatically reject him.

Saying he is not ready can also be a way of putting off a discussion of marriage, and many men use it to do just this. So when you ask a man why he is not ready, be wary if he refuses to discuss the subject. If he is of marriageable age, you need to put some diplomatic pressure on him. But before you start pressuring him, make sure he has thought about his answer. Women usually think about what they say—and then think a lot about what is said to them. Men often do not, and as a result they say things they do not mean and later regret.

When he says he isn't ready, find out if he really means it. Come back to the subject in a few days. You may find that it isn't the answer he wished he had given. Under the pressure of the moment, men often say one thing when they mean something else. But if "not ready" is his answer, and you decide to give him an ultimatum, how you go about it will affect how he responds. Before you go to the "either/or" stage, make sure you understand the man's answer.

One man we met two minutes after obtaining a marriage license had given the "not ready" answer three weeks earlier. Luckily, his fiancée asked why. He told her he was moving out of his bachelor pad and buying a house; he wanted to have a place with a room for her five-year-old son before asking her to marry him. Another gentleman, when he told his girlfriend he was working as a troubleshooter for his company and would be traveling every week for the next nine months, said he was not rejecting her. He didn't think he should get married while he was working on the road so much of the time; it wouldn't be fair to his wife. A third man told us he hadn't thought he was earning enough to support a wife, but he was looking for a job that paid better. The woman he was going with dumped him without talking to him about his problem and how he planned to solve it. I met him a year and a half later coming out of the marriage license bureau in New York City with the woman he dated after being dumped. He had just started working as a firefighter.

. . . Or Else

There are several ways of telling a man "either/or." The least effective method is to challenge him—*either you do this, or I do that.* Most men react negatively to direct challenges. They take on challenges. They don't like being pushed around, particularly by the woman in their life. If you force a man into a corner, most of the time his response is not going to be positive. If you tell most men you're going to start looking for someone else, they'll tell you to go ahead, and the relationship will self-destruct. After interviewing hundreds of women who received what they perceived as a negative answer and turned it into a yes, I'm convinced the indirect approach is by far the best.

The most common indirect approach is to let the emotional moment go by. Come back to the subject when he's not feeling defensive. One woman who was in sales suggested picking a time when he's in a good mood; it's always easier, she observed, to sell something to a person in a good mood. When you bring up the subject again, tell him directly that his answer hurt and upset you. You thought this relationship was going somewhere. If you get no response, you can then add that you're going to have to seriously think about the relationship. Don't say you've made up your mind to leave him if he says no. Make it clear you aren't challenging him, but rather letting him know that you haven't found his answer satisfactory. Once you've hinted that you might leave him, drop the subject. Give him time to think about what you've said.

The women we talked to who were about to marry told the men they had to think about their relationship because they wanted to have a husband and children. After telling the men what they wanted out of life, the women didn't press it any further. Sometimes that worked. When it did not, they hinted that if he could not give them what they wanted, they might have to look for somebody who could. Almost all the women added that they had been hoping to spend their life with him, or that they wanted him to be the father of their children, or that they loved him and leaving would break their hearts, and so forth.

Most women who turned an "I am not ready" or "I don't think I'm going to get married" into a "yes" sent one critical message:

I love you, but I need marriage.

The central message was that they really cared for their man, but they didn't let him off the hook. They said things such as, "I'm hurt that you don't think enough of me to marry me." Almost all these women became very upset and showed it.

If the range of emotional answers were to be put on the scale of 1 to 10, we had one that was an 11. We were interviewing couples in the Midwest when we ran across Terry and Joe.

Joe was one of the most affable people I have ever met. He seemed to smile all the time; most of the time, in fact, he looked as if he was about to break into laughter. He had the group in hysterics when he told the story of how he proposed to Terry.

Terry, as she served Joe dinner in her apartment, asked him in a whisper if he had ever thought about getting married. Although he didn't take his eyes off the TV, she knew he heard the question, because he murmured, "I guess not." He had never thought about marriage, and he did not want to think about it. The minute his answer sank in, she started screaming at him. She told him he wasn't smart enough to walk and chew gum at the same time. To give her an answer like that was insulting and stupid, and furthermore, he didn't deserve her. She added, "Without much effort, I could get someone smarter, richer, and better looking than you." She continued: "I wish I weren't in love with you, because you're a dumb ass." During this entire one-sided conversation, which she carried on at the top of her lungs, he continued to watch a football game. When Joe did not respond, Terry started throwing his things out her sixth-story window. That got his attention. Knowing he'd said the wrong thing, Joe didn't try to stop her when she threw his electric shaver, a couple of shirts, and a tie into the street. It was only when Terry took his $550 suit out of the closet that he finally assured her he'd gotten the message. Joe then wrapped his arms around Terry and said, "If you want to get married that badly, we'll get married. Just stop throwing things out the window—you could kill somebody."

That didn't calm her down. Terry said, "You act like you're doing me a favor. I'm doing you a favor!" When he agreed with her, she started to calm down. Terry sat on her couch crying and saying over and over, "How dare you say that?" It finally dawned on Joe that his answer had really hurt her, so Joe said, "If you want to whack me, go ahead. I have it coming." Then he told us, with an expression of feigned surprise and pain, "Do you know what she did? She hit me right in the nose." He was six foot five and powerfully built, while she was five foot two and weighed 110 pounds at most. Then Joe announced that he was running out to buy Terry a ring because he feared for his life.

Now, Terry and Joe were an unusual pair; I wouldn't recommend that if your man says he's never thought about marriage, you throw his property into the street or punch him in the nose. But I do think you should let him know how much he has hurt and offended you. There should be no question in his mind at the end of the conversation that you're devastated. The difference between women who received this answer and turned it into a yes and the women who accepted it was that they responded unambiguously and emotionally. They all seemed to have made the same two points:

> ➤ "How could you do this to me? You hurt me."

> ➤ "The reason I'm so hurt is that I love you."

Those two points were repeated over and over by the women we met coming out of marriage license bureaus. I can't tell you that this always produces the desired result, but it was the most common reaction among women about to marry. Women in love become very emotional when the man they love disappoints them, and many men respond positively to the force and honesty of such a response. It is one path to getting a yes.

Looking for Love in Other Places

There is another way of answering the man in your life who says he does not want—or is not ready—to marry you. And that is simply to say nothing, but to start looking elsewhere. We talked to a number of women who said they did this, including women who were living with men at the time. These women were coming out of marriage license bureaus. A dozen of the men dating the women said they realized the women were leaving or thinking of leaving them. They started noticing when their partners came home late. They also noticed that they started buying new clothing, losing weight, and going out with the girls at night. The men were convinced that the women were looking to replace them, and that's why they proposed.

We are also sure there were men who ended relationships when they realized their partners were looking around. That's a chance a woman takes.

A number of women coming out of marriage license bureaus reported the men's response in discussing marriage included "Not now," "I don't want to discuss it," "Marriage isn't in my lifestyle," "I need my space," or simply "Good-bye." After a period of two or three weeks, the men missed the women so much they proposed.

A classic example was Jeff and Sarah. They had been going together about two years when Jeff took Sarah to his sister's wedding. The wedding took place at ten-thirty in the morning, and the reception didn't start until almost two in the afternoon. While the bride and groom were having their pictures taken, most of the wedding party went out and had a few drinks. By the time they got to the reception, Jeff and Sarah were a bit less inhibited than usual. Sarah leaned over and asked Jeff: "Do you ever think about us getting married?" Jeff did not agree, but she said his answer was, word for word: "I haven't thought about it at all."

Jeff then turned to listen to the bandleader, who was doing standard wedding humor. When he turned back, Sarah was gone. He went looking for her, but she had disappeared. Finally he called her apartment. Sarah answered the telephone but hung up on him. He tried calling back, but every time he called she hung up. Finally, the phone was busy all the time. Jeff presumed she took it off the hook. Jeff stayed at his sister's wedding reception for another hour or two and then headed for her apartment. He was knocking on the door when two police officers came up behind him. Sarah told the officers she didn't want Jeff banging on her door, and they asked him to leave.

Over the next week, he returned to her place several times, and he kept calling. No matter how hard he tried, he could not contact her. She finally deigned to speak to him after he sent her an engagement ring via FedEx with a written marriage proposal and an apology. When we interviewed Sarah, she said she was still angry about the response he gave her at the reception.

How dare he, at his sister's wedding, tell her that he wasn't even considering marrying her? Sarah, after assuring me she was nonviolent, said she actually thought of picking up the centerpiece and crowning Jeff.

More than a hundred men and women we interviewed coming out of the marriage license bureaus told us that they had been in previous relationships that had progressed to the point where marriage was discussed. In most of these cases, the man's initial reaction to the topic was negative. Most of the women reacted to these negative responses by telling the man: *Marry me or get lost.* More than half the men said that when faced with only those choices, their pride forced them to get lost. Similarly, most of the time, when a woman walked out on a man, he let her go. Sometimes confrontations work, but not very often.

If I had discovered a nice, neat formula that would let women know when or even if they should say "either/or," I would have put it on the first page. Unfortunately, there is no such formula for handling men; they're too complicated and diverse.

On a number of occasions we interviewed and ran focus groups with women who were in their late thirties and forties who were not married and didn't believe they would marry. One of the characteristics of these women was that they were often in long-term dead-end relationships. When a man convinces a woman there is no prospect their relationship will lead to marriage, she should end the relationship—that is, if she has a desire to be married. Women in "go-nowhere" relationships should end them as soon as possible, because every year a woman stays in that kind of relationship dramatically decreases her chances of marrying. When we interviewed the young women coming out of marriage license bureaus, the one thing on which most all agreed was that if a woman was in a relationship that she was convinced would not lead to the altar, the best thing to do was break it off.

We ran several focus groups with women about to marry, and the consensus of these women was that women who let themselves stay in dead-end relationships were fearful. Many of these women said it took courage to do the right thing, but courage is one of the things you need in this world if you want to succeed. If you want to succeed in business, or in life, you have to have the backbone to do what needs to be done. On the other hand, some of the same women explained that it's a lot more difficult for a woman to break up with a man than the reverse. They thought the emotional attachment a woman has is much deeper than that of a man, and this makes breaking up with someone she deeply cares for a very painful experience.

The brides as a group, however, advised women in dead-end relationships to break them off immediately. The trick is to do it as soon as you know. The more you delay, the more difficult it becomes. One woman put it very colorfully. She said being with someone is like digging a hole. The longer you dig, the deeper the hole becomes, and the harder it is to get out.

Many women who want to marry are their own worst enemies. They either let men string them along, or they string themselves along with unrealistic hopes. If after you take reasonable steps to get a man to propose, you become convinced that he'll never do it, you're probably right. Even if he marries someone else after breaking up with you, don't question your judgment, because there are many reasons a man marries one woman and not another. His background may have made it impossible for him to commit to you; when he was dating you he was not ready emotionally, financially, or chronologically; the timing was not right, or he was convinced the marriage would not work; or any of a hundred other reasons that defy logic.

Once you're convinced your relationship is going nowhere, you should ask yourself two questions. Is this relationship so satisfying that I choose it over trying to find a man who will marry me? If your answer is yes, you must ask a second question. Since he won't commit to marriage, what are the chances that the relationship will last five, ten, or twenty years? We interviewed a number of unmarried women in their late thirties, forties, and fifties who chose to stay with a man they knew would not marry them on the assumption that they would be always be together. In a majority of cases, the women made the decision when they were still young enough to move in the singles world, which makes meeting men easier. Many of the men in these long-term relationships left the women for someone younger.

Marriage remains the formula for the best and longest-lasting relationships. Men are most likely to marry after carefully considering all possibilities. However, since men hardly ever speak about marriage, you must first get them talking about it if you want them to think about it.

Reversals

We did run across a small number of men who changed their minds after saying yes, or virtually saying yes. Most did so for a couple of reasons. The first was that they had spoken without thinking; after they had time to think, they said, they changed their minds. A few told us they had made the commitment after a few drinks, and when the liquor wore off, they knew they had made a mistake. Still, an equal number of men who broke off engagements told us that the women took "The idea appeals to me" to mean "Let's pick a date" or acted as if "Now that you've made the commitment, I own you." Or, "You have nothing more to say; all you have to do is show up."

They were frightened, particularly when the women instantly made those or similar assumptions as soon as the words were out of their mouths. We met these men coming out of marriage license bureaus, and even though they were marrying someone else, most of them agreed they might have married the first woman if she had not overwhelmed them. So whatever you do:

> *If a man tells you he finds the idea of marrying very appealing, give him time before discussing your wedding or your future together.*

There is no formula for these proposals. The stories of how happy couples decide to marry are almost as numerous as the couples who tell them. I hope recounting a few will give you some idea of the ways people decide to marry. Some couples were so determined to marry that from the moment they first discussed the subject of their wedding day, they planned every step almost like a military campaign. Others seemed to fall accidentally into marriage, while most were a combination of accident and planning.

What a majority had in common is that they knew where they were headed from the beginning. One couple who come to mind are Charles and Lisa. We met outside the marriage license bureau in Boston. They told me they had first discussed getting married two or three nights earlier when they were sitting in his car in front of her house. She was about to go in when he casually mentioned he would like to marry her. In her mind, he had not proposed; he had not even made a real commitment. As she saw it, he'd only speculated that they would make a terrific married couple. She was convinced that they were going to get married, but she was waiting for his formal proposal. Charles, however, thought he had proposed, and since she hadn't objected, he assumed she accepted. He arranged to take a day off so they could go to the marriage license bureau, then ran out and bought a ring. Four days later, I was interviewing them in front of the marriage license bureau at 11 A.M. Charles told me he would answer my questions, but I would have to hurry—he had the day planned: a romantic lunch, a show in the afternoon, and a celebration that evening. This couple was atypical. The man made all the assumptions and did most of the planning. Like the other couples in this category, however, they knew from the minute he broached the subject that they were headed to the altar.

Making a List

The next couple was very typical, not only because the woman did the planning but because they got their marriage license despite being very busy. The young woman had a checklist, as do many women when they walk into a marriage license bureau. When they picked up the marriage license, she checked it off.

Mike was thirty and Julie was twenty-eight when they met at a mutual friend's apartment. Both said that after years in the singles scene they were cautious, but after a few months they decided this was special. They had been going out for about a year and a half when he proposed. Although she had not expected him to show up with a ring on an ordinary Friday night, his proposal was not a surprise. They had talked about marriage several times and more or less agreed about most things. Mike got the message that Julie wanted him to commit; according to Mike, she dropped hints just often enough to get his attention but not often enough to annoy him. She said she never brought up the subject when he was watching TV or a movie because she knew it drove him crazy.

Mike proposed as soon as he entered her apartment because he had left the champagne and chocolates in the hall and was afraid they'd disappear if he waited too long. They spent the evening drinking champagne, eating chocolates, and calling friends and family.

Possibly the reason Mike proposed was that Julie had good instincts. The men we spoke to said a woman dropping hints didn't bother them unless they were delivered at an inappropriate time or place—when they were watching TV, when there were other people around, when he was in the middle of some project, when he was driving, and so forth. Several were walking out of a marriage license bureau with women who had not pestered them. One woman told us that she dropped hints only when she handed her fiancé a drink. It was a trick she had learned from her mother, who asked her father for things only when giving him his second martini. But you don't need alcohol to make the principle work for you. The best time to discuss marriage is when men are engaged in activities that bring them pleasure and are, as a result, relaxed and in a good humor.

In Over Their Heads

While few marriages are canceled because the bride and groom can't agree on wedding plans, it does happen. When we talked to people who broke up after getting engaged, three things became clear. First, the men who broke up with their brides did not cut them enough slack. They did not understand that a young woman who had never planned anything bigger than an informal party for friends was now planning an extravagant wedding, which can be as complex as putting on a TV awards show. This takes real management skills, which most brides do not have. In over her head and feeling tremendous pressure, the average woman will become a bit sharp and occasionally unreasonable.

Second, the bride forgets why she is marrying the man and starts treating him shabbily, or worse, ignores him.

Third, one or the other gets cold feet, and there is no one to explain to them that most brides and grooms have moments of doubt.

After talking to hundreds of newly married couples and a few who did not make it to the altar, I suggest that couples anticipate the inevitable fights, shouting matches, and cold feet that are likely to take place during this very stressful time. They must agree before they start that they aren't going to let such things destroy the whole purpose of planning a wedding.

Statistical Truths, Speaking of Marriage

➤ Women who discuss marriage at least know where they stand.

➤ Men who discuss marriage are more likely to propose.

➤ If you want to discuss marriage, you're probably going to have to bring the subject up, because many men never will.

➤ More than 73 percent of women coming out of marriage license bureaus said they put pressure on their man to get him to propose.

➢ If a woman is convinced that marriage is essential to her happiness, she is more likely to marry.

➢ If a man is convinced that being married is essential to a woman's happiness, he is more likely to ask her to marry him.

➢ When a man who has been going with a woman for months says he has not thought about marriage, there is a good chance he's just being honest.

➢ Men usually don't get subtle hints—a woman has to discuss marriage directly and, to make sure he gets the point, ask follow-up questions.

➢ When a man says he is not ready to marry, he is speaking in the moment—it usually doesn't mean he will never marry.

➢ Men rarely respond positively when challenged.

➢ Women are often their own worst enemies.

6

Marrying After Forty

IN THE LATE 1980s, a study was published that claimed a forty-year-old woman was more likely to be killed by terrorists than to marry.* (This study took place before September 11, 2001, when terrorist attacks were rarer than lighting strikes.) At the time, it caused quite a stir and was the topic of the day on talk shows and at office watercoolers. The minute I heard about it, I pulled out my copy of the U.S. Census Bureau statistical abstract and found that almost 9 percent of the women who married in 1980 were over forty. I remember a discussion I had at the time with two female researchers in their early forties. I wondered aloud how such a ridiculous statement could be a topic of debate among intelligent women.

Both researchers gave virtually the same answer: They had single friends in their forties who found it terribly difficult to meet eligible men, so they were convinced the study had a ker-

---

*This study, published in *Newsweek* (June 2, 1986) by Yale sociologists Neil Bennett and Patricia H. Craig and Harvard economist David E. Bloom, concluded that white college-educated women born in the mid-1950s had only a 20 percent chance of marrying at age thirty-five, and that forty-year-olds, with a minuscule 2.6 percent probability of tying the knot, were more likely to be killed by a terrorist than to marry.

nel of truth in it. Some accepted it because it gave them an excuse to quit the singles scene, which they found uncomfortable. One woman explained she had a younger unmarried sister whose reaction to the study was to give up on the idea of marrying. She said she no longer felt obliged to go to the stupid singles places anymore. This woman told us she literally pushed her sister out the door on Friday night. She said, "I will not allow her to give up on life as long as there's a real chance she'll find someone, and I think there is." Since I had just finished reading the census figures on marriage, I agreed with her and told her so.

Although I'm firmly convinced that the search for a husband after age forty is anything but futile, I feel obliged to report three facts our research uncovered:

> ➤ The chances that you will find a man are less than they were when you were younger. That is a statistical fact. The pool of available men gets smaller as a woman gets older. But there *are* still eligible men— so read on.

> ➤ Men look at the world differently as they get older. Some women get trapped in the past and are disappointed because they expect men to respond to them the same way they did when they were in their twenties and thirties. It's unlikely that men will come flocking to you; for most women over forty, that isn't a realistic expectation. A majority of women with steady boyfriends started dating them as a result of efforts on their part. Women must be more proactive, not more passive, once they turn forty.

> Luck plays a part. But as any multimillionaire Las Vegas casino owner will testify, if you can arrange the odds so that they are in your favor, you can make your own luck.

Women over forty looking for husbands said they faced three main challenges:

> First, it was difficult to meet eligible men.

> Second, they believed all the good ones had been taken.

> Third, men their age were dating and marrying twenty- and thirty-year-olds, and there was no way they could compete with these youngsters.

While our studies showed that these challenges were sometimes real, we also saw they were obstacles that could be maneuvered around.

Meeting Men

There is no question that it is often difficult for women over forty to meet eligible men. In fact, it is hard for most women over thirty-six to meet eligible men, because they no longer move with ease in the singles scene.

Our questioning of engaged women over forty showed that a majority, including those who met their men in other ways, thought the best way to meet a future husband was through friends. This is one of the great misconceptions held by women. Without a doubt, it's how most women get their dates—but it isn't necessarily how they get their husbands.

At least 64 percent of the dates women over forty have are with men they meet through friends. In most cases, it is a setup. These setups range from elaborate dinner parties thrown for the sole purpose of seating two people together with the hope they'll click, to chance introductions at work.

Interestingly, while almost two-thirds of the dates that women over forty have come from setups, less than one-third of marriages result from these arranged meetings. It's easy to see why: When men and women meet at unplanned social functions, they evaluate each other, immediately eliminating undesirables and making dates only with good prospects for a relationship. Since a woman can't prescreen blind dates or setups, she's likely to have to date from four to six men before she finds a promising one.

If you can arrange to meet men in social settings, it increases the probability that a casual date will lead to a relationship that might lead to marriage. Of the women over forty who were about to be married, almost a third said they met their fiancés in social settings.

Easier Said Than Done

That is an amazing statistic, because there are very few places for people over forty to meet. Unfortunately, for the most part, there are few forty-plus singles groups associated with churches, and for many people when they were younger, that was the primary place they went to meet members of the opposite sex. The most obvious places to meet are bars. Most of the women we talked to said they were not comfortable in bars. Nevertheless, there are cocktail lounges where the crowd tends to be single and older. There are also cruises and a few resorts that cater to older singles, but not nearly enough. In fact, a travel business that would organize outings for single men and women between the ages of forty and fifty-five would make a fortune. The people we interviewed said they would love to go on a trip or to a resort where the youngest woman would be thirty-six and the youngest man would be forty. Few such resorts exist—if there were more, they would probably be booked all the time.

Until those places come along, however, outside of a few singles cocktail lounges, the best place to meet men is in clubs—but not just any clubs. If you want to meet single men your age, join clubs whose membership includes a substantial number of single men. Since single men over forty usually have far more money than twenty-somethings, they're most likely to be found at clubs that cater to an affluent crowd. Joining any club with an upper-middle-class membership—a yacht club, a tennis club, a country club—will probably help. Even if most of its members are married, with today's divorce rate you'll find eligible men in most clubs.

At the top of the list, however, are athletic clubs. When we were in our twenties, many of us drank too much, ate too much, and kept ungodly hours without it showing. We looked great in spite of ourselves. That is the advantage of youth. As we get a bit older, most of us start to put on weight—and often go to gyms to do something about it.

This is why 21 percent of the women over forty whom we met with their fiancés told us that they had met their partners in clubs dedicated to activities that helped keep the members in shape, such as gyms, ski clubs, swim clubs, and bicycling clubs.

After joining a club and looking around, you may conclude you've made a mistake if you don't meet anyone right away. Don't give up. You may have joined the wrong club, but until you visit the club at different times, you can't be sure. Often such clubs offer trial memberships at reduced rates, which enable you to preview the clientele before making the big investment.

We met many women over forty who told us they joined a specific club solely to keep in shape. Only after they were members for a while did they discover there were older singles in the club as well.

Getting into the Swim

The best example was Joan, who at forty-six had been a member of a swim club for four years. She went Monday, Tuesday, Wednesday, and Thursday mornings before work and swam for half an hour. Joan said it was great exercise, and she loved it. Her primary reason for swimming was to stay in shape.

Joan was a divorced mom with two teenage boys who had reached the age when they didn't want to go on vacations with her or even talk to her. She said her kids grunted "Yeah" and "Nah" when she tried to have a conversation with them. She was lonely, and she wanted to meet a man. An accountant, she had joined several professional organizations, but she said she never thought of the swim club as a place to meet men. One morning Joan left her purse in a locker, so she stopped off at the swim club after work to pick it up. Since she was there anyway, she decided to swim that evening and sleep for an extra half hour in the morning. After she finished her laps, she sat on the side of the pool to catch her breath.

In less than five minutes, Joan was approached by two men. She didn't know what was going on; in fact, it startled her. But after talking to a couple of the women, Joan understood. After eight o'clock, the pool and the adjacent snack area were filled with older singles. The women referred to it as "the meet market." They said they met men there all the time. For them it was an over-forty singles place. Most of the members with day jobs swam in the morning or after work. Those who were married went home to be with their families, while the singles hung around or arrived late. This very sophisticated lady met her fiancé at the pool, and two other women she knew met their husbands there.

Joan's experience was typical in several ways. She met her fiancé in a club where the members exercised. She was not aware when she first joined the club that there was a singles group at the club or that it was made up mostly of older singles. Finally, the singles group was not an official part of the club but an unofficial gathering that took place at a specific time and in a specific place. It was like a club within a club. After interviewing dozens of women who met men under similar circumstances, we started to look at clubs. First, we looked at clubs where our researchers were members. After we discovered that half their clubs had a built-in singles scene, we added questions about club membership to all our questionnaires.

What we discovered was that:

> Sports clubs dedicated to activities that attract singles—trips, bicycling—are the best place to meet eligible men over forty.

> Next best are sports clubs—tennis, golf—that attract a large number of singles.

> Third best are nonathletic professional or social organizations whose members are overwhelmingly men, such as associations of engineers, accountants, or collectors of sports memorabilia.

> ➤ After those clubs came organizations with the normal percentage of married and single men and women that have a singles scene: the nineteenth hole at a golf club on Friday nights, the tennis class on Tuesday nights.

> ➤ Organizations that sponsor events offer single members a chance to socialize with other club members; dances, picnics, and charity golf or tennis tournaments are also wonderful places to meet men.

Let your interests be your guide. Don't allow the list above to limit your options. One woman we interviewed was an avid bridge player and met her fiancé at a bridge tournament. She said she had not played serious bridge in years, but because a lot of men play tournament bridge, she brushed up her game. We also interviewed dozens of women who took up golf because playing helped in business—and they also found that it helped them meet men. These women told us that at most golf clubs most of the men are married, but they pointed out that there are always single members.

Go where the men are.

Boys' Toys

Another example of a woman joining a men's group was Megan. Four years earlier, when we met her coming out of a marriage license bureau, she was a forty-eight-year-old antique-toy dealer who specialized in dolls. Megan had given up on finding Mr. Right. One weekend she rented space at an antique-toy show, which was a normal part of her business. At these shows she sold dolls from her shop and occasionally purchased dolls for her collection. Once Megan was inside, she realized she had made a mistake: Most of the dealers were selling model trains. Megan left after she became convinced she was wasting her time—but she couldn't help noticing that the place was full of men. Two years later she was at a toy auction, and six sets of trains were put up for bid. She put in a lowball bid on the first set, never expecting to get it. To her surprise, she ended up with all six sets.

When the next model-train show came to town, she rented space to sell the train sets. Once she opened her booth, her neighbors at the show introduced themselves, and she became part of that train group. To her surprise, the place was full of single men, and one asked her for a date. Megan didn't go out with him—mainly, she said, because he had caught her off guard. But she went to the next four local model-train shows and did date the third, fourth, and fifth men who asked. She had not had a date in three years, and she started having so much fun she set a part of her shop aside to sell trains.

When we asked her if she had any advice for women her age, Megan said, "If they want to meet men, tell them to buy or sell model trains. Men come attached to them." Although overstated, her message is valid. If you want to meet men, join a group whose membership is overwhelmingly male.

Dipping Your Pen in the Company Ink

Statistically, the third best place (after athletic and social clubs) for women over forty to meet men is through work. Don't be discouraged if you've never met a man at work. The reason may be that you're treating the workplace the way you did when you were in your twenties. Many people in their twenties and some in their thirties never date anyone from work; they've bought into the common wisdom that it can create problems and just isn't worth it. If you believe that, you might want to reexamine your thinking.

Once you reach forty, it is far more difficult to meet eligible men. Most of your single friends who used to help you meet men are married, and their new friends are usually married couples. It's very important that you maintain friends and contacts from your business life. The reason for these friendships doesn't disappear once the other party is married. To start, you should get to know as many people in your business as possible. Don't limit yourself to people in your department or even in your company. Seeking friends at work is a win–win game: It helps your career to have contacts in your company, in your industry, and with your clients. These contacts also become invaluable in maintaining an active social life after your single friends marry.

There may be someone in the next department you would love to meet and who would love to meet you. If there is, in all probability neither of you knows the other one exists, and you'll never meet unless someone goes out of his or her way to introduce you. That's why it's preferable to have female friends in your company and field. Male friends, even when they get older, are far less likely to set women up than female friends. To be more specific, the friends who are most likely to introduce you to eligible men are single women your age and at your level. If you're an engineer, it would be smart to make an effort to socialize with other single female engineers, accountants, executives, and so forth. You should also become friends with as many married women at work as possible; they're your second best resource for meeting men at work. Men in offices almost never arrange for people to meet.

Get Out There!

One of the characteristics of women who marry after forty is that they have a large number of female friends over forty who are willing to help them meet men. These unofficial confederations are quite successful in helping women keep their social lives active.

Having an active social life is very important if you want to marry after forty. Women over forty who live by themselves, whose daily routine is to go to work in the morning, come home at night, eat alone, watch TV, and go to bed every night for months at a time, are not likely to meet anyone they would like to marry.

➢ Women who make it a point to go out at least two nights every week, even if they simply eat with other women or do volunteer work, are three times more likely to marry than those who stay at home.

➢ Those who go out three times a week are more likely to marry than those who go out twice a week.

➢ For some odd reason, going out more than five nights a week appears to decrease a woman's chances of marrying. Maybe she's not home to answer the phone.

Having Faith

Many women meet their future husbands by accident. Nancy, who was in her early fifties and had been a widow for twelve years, believed it was faith, not fate, that teamed her with Grant. She was a devout Christian and told us she prayed she would meet someone on a company trip. Nancy was convinced her prayer had been answered. She said no other explanation would make sense.

Nancy was at a convention in Puerto Rico when she ran into a group of women in her hotel lobby getting ready to go on a bus trip to a rain forest. She signed up because she had nothing better to do that afternoon. Fifteen minutes later, Nancy realized she was on a tour with a group of lesbians.

Nancy said she felt very uncomfortable and out of place. In the bus on the way back from the rain forest, a woman sat down next to her and said, "Relax, we all know you're straight." She went on to explain that her brother had accompanied her to Puerto Rico to get in on the group rates, but since the hotel was out in the country and filled with lesbians and computer geeks, he had eaten alone every night since they arrived. She asked if Nancy would like to have dinner with a nice man. Nancy and that very nice man spent that evening and the next day together, discovering that not only did they get along, but they also lived only about an hour and a half apart. When we interviewed them nine months and seventeen days later in Chicago, they had just bought an engagement ring.

While you shouldn't underestimate the power of prayer, Nancy's story teaches another truth: The more social contacts a woman has, no matter who they are, the better are her chances of meeting men. And the more men she meets, the better her chances of meeting that special one.

Interestingly enough, people over forty who described themselves as religious or churchgoers were much more likely to marry than those who did not, possibly because their religion teaches that living together without marriage is sinful, emphasizing the sanctity of marriage. For whatever reason, men and women who regularly attend church are more likely to marry over forty than those who do not.

All the Good Ones Are Taken

The second complaint that women have is, "All the good ones are taken." The real problem that many women over forty have in developing relationships is that they are still looking at men the way they did in high school. The ideal man is the star football player. They continue to pursue men who are tall and good-looking with a full head of hair. Most men, as they get older, put on weight and lose some if not all of their hair and boyish good looks. Women are constantly complaining about men being shallow; they gripe about men being interested only in how a woman looks and claim that's why many men in their forties and fifties go after twenty-year-olds. In fact, many women turn down older men for similar reasons. The men don't fit the picture they developed in high school or in their twenties of the ideal husband. Unfortunately, fewer and fewer men continue to look like the man of a woman's dreams as they grow older—and some never did. When this subject was brought up, women always denied a man's looks played such an important part in their decision making. But when we asked them whether they would date a man several inches shorter than they, or one who had a lisp, most admitted they might have a problem with either. These same women who claimed to be seriously looking for good men eventually admitted they have probably passed up some very good men because of minor physical or social flaws.

You don't need to disregard your standards or even significantly lower them. Rather, set realistic standards. Some of the same women who mock men for picking only gorgeous babes in their twenties refuse to date a man who lacks polish, whose taste is all in his mouth, who isn't a snappy dresser, or who doesn't know how to order wine in a restaurant. It is a simple fact that many single men over forty have limited social graces.

I'm not suggesting that women team up with men who are totally unsuitable:

> ➤ If a man drinks too much, uses drugs, or has never held a steady job, don't even consider him as husband material.
> ➤ If he still lives with Mom, you may have to forget him.
> ➤ Any man who ever threatens physical violence should be avoided like the plague.

But when a woman's only reason for turning down a man is that his social graces are not up to her standards, she may be making a mistake.

We met dozens of men who admitted to having limited social skills when they met their future brides but who had improved in that area as a result of meeting their fiancées. If a man is basically a decent person who shares your values, date him a few times. Find out if he's willing to learn how to conduct himself in a way that pleases you. Many men we met said they'd be happy to acquire a bit more polish. Surprisingly, once men hit a certain age, they are generally not as sensitive to criticism as they had been in their youth. These men not only listened to their fiancées and wives but actually bragged about the social skills the women had taught them. It was just another way of touting their own good judgment in choosing a wife.

Finding a Jewel in a Pigpen

Three women from Texas provide a classic story of women writing men off too quickly. All three lived in the same apartment building, two in one apartment and the other down the hall. One was a lawyer, another was head of public relations at a retail store, and the third a comptroller at the same store. They referred to the apartment across from the attorney's apartment as "the pigpen." Several men lived in that apartment. One day when they had left their door open, one of the women peeked inside and saw stuff strewn all over the place. These three very sophisticated women agreed that the men were not the type any of them would ever date. When I asked them what had convinced them these men were losers, the only specific thing they mentioned was that all three men went to work wearing jeans and baseball caps.

I was hired by the department store chain where two of the women worked to help open a new store. I spoke on "Dressing for Success" twice, once for the public and once for the store employees. During the question-and-answer period with the employees, I used a part of my research on marriage to illustrate a point. Once I mentioned the marriage research, I was bombarded with questions. I cut them off by promising that after the presentation, I would summarize the research on marriage and answer questions.

After a postspeech session that lasted more than two hours, the three Texas women met for dinner. The subject of conversation was the marriage research. Only half in earnest, they decided that since they would all be forty in less than three years, they would lower their standards a little bit. The lawyer, tongue in cheek, suggested that the only way to demonstrate their new standards was for one of them to date one of the men from the pigpen. They were just kidding around, but they did make a serious bet. The first one to go out with a man from the pigpen would win a hundred dollars from each of the other two. That night each put a hundred-dollar check into a jar. They told me they laughed about it for months, waving the jar in each other's faces. The "pigpen" men had made passes at all of them when they had first moved into the building. The women had turned them down, and the men stopped pursuing them rather than face further rejection.

Two months later, the accountant announced to her two friends that in a week she would own the jar. She had a date with a man from the pigpen. One of the pigpen men had approached her in the elevator. When he asked her to go out with him, instead of turning him down flat, she wanted to know where they would go. When he named one of the better restaurants in town, she accepted. What worried her afterward was that she'd never seen the man in a tie, and she knew he'd need to wear a jacket and a tie to get into that restaurant. Even though she had talked to him for only a few minutes, he had seemed nice, and she didn't want him to be embarrassed. She would have backed tactfully out of the date, but she knew her friends would never let her live it down.

When they showed up at the fine restaurant, something very strange happened. The maître d' pushed the line aside, put his arm around her date's shoulder, and made a big fuss over him. He added, "We've got your coat and tie waiting."

Then he walked them back to a section of the restaurant she didn't know existed, which was like a private dining room.

They had a wonderful time. He was funny and entertaining, and, to her surprise, she really liked him. When they got back to the apartment, he thanked her for a great evening, gave her a polite kiss, and said good night.

The next day at work she did some inquiring and discovered he had started several computer companies. Apparently he held several patents, and computer makers paid him every time they used his inventions. In addition, he and his partners developed advanced computers for the Pentagon. It turned out one of the men who shared the pigpen with him was his partner, and the other worked with him on various projects. He stayed in this apartment because it was close to the office. He had a very large home in an upscale suburb that he had bought when he was married but seldom used. He had been divorced seven years earlier and had apparently given his first wife millions. He was easy to research—everything he'd done had been reported in a local gossip column or on the business pages of the two local papers.

I met this couple on their way to pick up a marriage license fourteen months later. The woman's two friends were dating men they had met through him.

Some of Your Best Friends Are Guys

I pointed out earlier that having male friends really isn't a significant factor in finding a husband when you're in your twenties and early thirties. Having contacts with men when you're over forty, however, can be a godsend. Once men reach forty, most of them find it difficult to meet women, and as a result they are much more understanding of a woman's position. If a woman friend says she would like to meet a man they know, often they will go out of their way to set up the meeting. Younger men usually will not.

Men Dating Younger Women

The third problem that women over forty complained about was that men their age wanted to date and marry women in their twenties and thirties. There is some truth in this; we regularly ran across men between forty and forty-six marrying women in their twenties and thirties.

Life isn't fair. Men over forty have more options than women the same age. When they are in their twenties and thirties, men usually marry women who are two to four years younger. By the time they reach their forties, the age difference is often greater. But in general, men tend to marry women close to their own age and with whom they have common interests. Common interests are at least in part a product of age.

Our surveys show that 90 percent of men over forty-four think of themselves as being too old for the singles scene. Most feel uncomfortable approaching women in their twenties and are hesitant to do so unless the woman signals them ahead of time that she's interested. In addition, almost half the men over forty who have dated, lived with, or married much younger women told us they would hesitate to do so again. These men said they were not comfortable in those relationships because the younger women wanted a different lifestyle, insisting on going to clubs or partying when their older partners wanted to hang around and watch TV. The women who had been in May–December relationships complained that the older men became jealous and made fools of themselves whenever they even talked to a younger man.

When we mentioned the jealousy issue to men, many admitted it was a problem. A substantial age difference creates so many additional problems that many couples who seem to be headed for the altar never get there.

> *This is why, although men often date women much younger than they are, they usually marry someone closer to their own age.*

Attracting Men Over Forty

Men are attracted by different things at different ages. When we asked men over forty what first attracted them to their fiancées, their most common answer was not that their fiancées were beautiful, were attractive, or had wonderful personalities (as men in their twenties and thirties pointed out), but that they took good care of themselves. Since more than half the men we questioned used the phrase *took care of herself,* we asked them why it was so important. Fifty-six percent said they had noticed that many women the age of their fiancées let themselves go. They wanted a woman who was going to stay in shape, keep her figure, and pay attention to her appearance.

One of the secrets of marrying when you are over forty is to be trim or athletic. If you have put on a few extra pounds, join a club—preferably one where you'll meet men, but definitely one where you'll lose weight and get in shape.

> *It's far more important to be in shape when you're dating in your forties than it was when you were in your twenties.*

In addition, while it is important for women to dress well and use makeup effectively when they are young, it's even more important after age forty. The women in this age range who men wanted to marry were usually well put together. The vast majority dressed well, styled their hair, and applied their makeup carefully.

The brides-to-be were better dressed and more carefully groomed than the women who did not marry. In fact, this was one of the primary differences between women over forty who married and those who did not.

Acts of Kindness

Interestingly, when we asked men in their twenties if there was one characteristic that first attracted them to the women they were marrying, most mentioned virtue, talent, or accomplishments. When we asked men over forty the same question, surprisingly, 62 percent said they were originally attracted to their fiancée because she was congenial, agreeable, relaxed, and easy to get along with. Without being asked, many of them gave specific examples of their fiancées being nice, either to them or to others.

Jimmy, a widower from South Carolina, told us about his first date with his future fiancée. They were walking along the street when she saw a woman holding two screaming kids and several packages. She excused herself, helped the woman over to her car, and strapped one of the kids in the car seat. The woman thanked her but was rather brusque. When she came back, Jimmy commented that the woman had not been very polite or grateful. She asked him if he had taken a good look at the mother's face; if he had, she said, he would have seen that she was under a lot of stress. Jimmy was so impressed by her kindness and sensitivity that for the first time since his wife had died six years earlier he thought he might marry again.

A divorced gentleman, Karl, told us that he met his wife, Jane, while working on his brother's campaign for sheriff. His brother had been in office for a number of years, but he was beaten by an unknown. His campaign workers were all upset on election night, and almost everyone at the headquarters had left. Karl said campaign headquarters after a victory is the place everyone wants to be, and after a defeat where no one wants to be. Since they were going to close the office the next day, his brother, his brother's wife, and two campaign workers were cleaning up. Papers, balloons, streamers, buttons, and signs were thrown all over the place. They were working half-heartedly when Jane came over. She yelled at his brother, the defeated sheriff, "What are you doing? Go home and have a couple of drinks. Get out of here, I'll clean the place up."

Karl said he liked Jane's assertive kindness so much he stayed with her. It was what had first attracted him.

Several men told us when they were sick, the women who later became their fiancées took care of them. One man we interviewed in Phoenix, Frank, told us that he had had the flu about a year earlier. At the time he had been dating his fiancée, Dina, for two months, and she had stayed over a couple of nights. Frank called Dina the night before to cancel their date for the next evening; he was too sick to get out of bed. He didn't expect to hear from her until he was on his feet. The next morning Frank was surprised when Dina showed up at seven-thirty with juice and soda. She got him out of bed, helped him to the couch, changed his sheets, put him back to bed again, and left for work. She returned that evening with soup and changed his sheets once again so he'd be comfortable. She changed his sheets a third time just before she left. She took the soiled sheets with her and showed up the next day with them laundered and folded. As he put it: "She came bearing soup, fruit juice, and clean sheets for three days." He said he never had such loving treatment all his life, and he vowed, "I'm going to marry you." She told him she liked him a lot, he was a nice guy, but she had been married and did not want to marry again. Ten months later, I met Frank and Dina on their way into the Phoenix marriage license bureau.

Mature men are often impressed when a woman is kind or considerate. Many have dated, lived with, or married women who were not kind or considerate, and experience has taught them that decency is more important than looks. Frank with the flu was typical. He had been married before, and his wife had never gone out of her way to be kind to him. Frank told us she was very beautiful and talented and expected to be treated like a princess all the time. He added that no matter how beautiful a woman is, adoring her constantly becomes a chore. That was why he had left her. So when a woman he had known for only two months went out of her way to be kind to him, he could not let her go.

What impressed most of these men was not that a woman pleased them but that she showed she really cared for them. One of the wealthiest couples I know, Ralph and Gina, had been married two years when I interviewed them in New York City. Before they married, Gina lived and worked in suburbia and could get into New York City only on weekends. Six months after they started going together, she was coming in almost every weekend and staying at Ralph's apartment in the city. When Gina's birthday came along, he went to Tiffany's and bought her a pearl necklace. He had never seen her wear a pearl necklace and assumed she didn't have one. On her birthday, he took her to a nice restaurant and gave her the necklace. She thanked him, put it on, and wore it home that night.

The next morning she said she was going to take Ralph to breakfast, but first she wanted to go shopping. Gina walked him to Tiffany's, handed him the pearls, and told him to get his money back, explaining that she already had a pearl necklace. He was a bit surprised, but he returned the pearls. Then she told him he wasn't off the hook: She still expected a birthday gift. He was getting angry, because he assumed she would pick out something more expensive than the necklace. Ralph really liked Gina, but he thought she was being very pushy. She took his hand and walked him through Tiffany's. He expected her to stop at every counter. Instead she walked out the other side of Tiffany's and up Madison Avenue for almost a mile to a store with espresso machines. Gina said she wanted an espresso machine, because Ralph had complained that his made muddy espresso, but he would never buy a new one.

Ralph had never before told Gina how impressed he'd been that she had traded a pearl necklace for an espresso machine they could share. Gina was startled to hear this and wanted to know why that had impressed him. Ralph said, "I'm not sure, but I thought, *Here's a woman who really likes me. It would be stupid of me to think my money didn't play some part in her attraction, but at least it's not all she wants.*"

Rich men, poor men, all men are impressed by acts that tell them someone really cares for them. This is particularly true of men over forty.

Compatible Lifestyles

Lifestyle means a great deal to men over forty. Most are set in their ways. Unless your social skills somehow match their lifestyle, they will in all probability find someone else. While you might find that many unmarried men after forty lack some social graces, you'll often find a fair share who are extremely successful and run in very dignified circles.

Men who marry after forty expect their brides to fit in with their business associates and friends, and they very seldom marry women whose style or behavior they find inappropriate. These qualities are too important for a man who has an established life. He'll add a woman to his life, but rarely will he trade his life for a woman.

Etiquette, always important, becomes more important the older we get. Read. Practice. It's never too late to improve your social graces.

Express Your Feelings

If you want to convince a man over forty that you're the woman for him, your first step is to let him know how you feel. You have to come right out and tell him you like him, love him, or want to marry him. Don't drop hints as women in their twenties and thirties are able to do; these men are beyond hints. They expect women to be up front with them. This is particularly true of men who have been married before. It's not that you should be the first to say "I love you" or the first to make a commitment, but if you have strong feelings for your man, let him know.

We spoke to more than a dozen men who had been going

out with women for years, and they wondered whether their women really loved them. We questioned their partners whenever we could, and every one of the women we talked to said of course she loved him, and of course he knew it. Many forty-plus men are very cautious and a bit cynical, so you need to tell them and show them you love them, sometimes over and over, before it sinks in.

Money Matters

We talked to men in their forties, fifties, and sixties who had been in relationships that seemed to be going somewhere but who had broken them off. When we asked them why, the main reason they gave was money. It wasn't always because they thought the women were after their money; what led to many breakups was that every time they brought up money, the women changed the subject. It made them nervous. We talked to a number of women who said that after going with a man for just a few months, he insisted on discussing her finances in detail. Many women, particularly women who had been married before, objected, as did some women who had assets of their own. Ironically, it made the women wonder if the men were interested in them or their money.

It's possible some of these men were primarily interested in the women's money. But almost one-third of the men over forty-five told us that before they committed to a serious relationship, they wanted to know what they were getting into. They thought they had the right to know what assets and debts the women had and that the women had the right to know what they had. Assuming both parties are being honest, such discussions should strengthen a relationship, not weaken it.

There's no reason to think that because a man wants to talk about finances, he must be in the relationship for money. It may mean he is being responsible. He has assets or obligations, or both, and he has to factor in what the woman is going to bring to the marriage before he decides what he's going to do.

It's also very worthwhile for women evaluating a potential mate to have this information. Between alimony and child support or other financial entanglements, marrying the wrong man can be a quick road to poverty.

Hot to Trot

The second most common reason women end promising relationships is that the men come on too quickly and scare them off. This is a major problem with the over-forty crowd. If after two or three months a man pushes for marriage, don't assume there's something wrong with him. Approximately 15 percent of men over forty try to rush their women to the altar. If you're interested in him, tell him the two of you need more time to get to know each other. Take it as a compliment, but hold off giving your answer for six months to a year. Most of the men who were dropped by women when they proposed early in the relationship said they would have waited, if asked. So ask. It will allow you to keep your options open and allow him to keep his self-respect and feelings intact.

Dying to Get Married

We talked to fifty-six single men over forty who were dying to get married. They represented approximately 11 percent of the singles we questioned in 1997 and 1998. Sixty-one percent of them admitted that when they met a woman for the first time, they were nervous and unsure of themselves. They told us they had been shot down so often, they were gun-shy. When we asked them why they wanted to marry, the answer most gave was they wanted what their brothers and friends had: "a normal life."

Half the men we talked to were with their fiancées, so we interviewed them as well. Nineteen of twenty-four women told us that when they first met the men they were about to marry, they had not been impressed. But woman after woman reported that once she got to know the man, she was crazy about him. Only four of the nineteen we questioned came to know their fiancés because they continued to date them; most worked with the men and were forced into repeated contact with them. Over and over, we heard that men who fell over their feet or got tangled up in their tongues when first meeting their fiancées turned out to be graceful and articulate once they relaxed, while others proved to be supernice guys.

You'll have to date a man who is socially inept at least half a dozen times before you get to see him as he is. It takes this long for men who have never been successful with women to relax and be themselves. By the same token, many men who have been married know exactly what to say and what buttons to push to please a woman. They'll be ideal companions for the first few dates, and you'll see the real man only after a dozen or more dates.

I recommend that after age forty, you date any man who seems like a decent person, and who obviously likes you, at least half a dozen times before giving up on him.

Forty-Plus Relationships

Relationships between people in their forties, fifties, and sixties are similar in many ways to the relationships between men and women in their twenties and thirties. Both groups progress through the same stages in their relationships. While the stages of relationships are similar, however, they are never identical.

Whether you are twenty-two or sixty-two, making a good first impression is important. No matter what your age, you want to announce nonverbally that you are positive, friendly, and fun. Men of all ages find women who send those three messages to be attractive. The best way for a young woman to send the message that she is upbeat and positive is to carry herself erectly. When you're over forty, an erect posture helps, but it isn't the primary way of announcing you're a positive person.

The most effective way for a woman over forty to send a positive message is verbally.

Couples over forty usually engage in serious discussions earlier in relationships than do couples in their twenties. They are more likely to spend time doing things that require conversation and an exchange of ideas. Twenty-year-olds, in contrast, often plan their dates around entertainment—movies, dancing, sailing. A twenty-year-old can be with a person for a considerable period without knowing much about him or her. That's usually not the case with the over-forty crowd. To send a positive message when you're over forty, you need to adopt a positive attitude or at least avoid making negative comments.

This is particularly important when you meet a man who is starting life anew. Starting life anew in one's forties and fifties is a phenomenon not limited to men who have just divorced or become widowers, but it is more common to them than any other group. Whether their first wife dies or leaves them, or they leave her, doesn't matter; nor does whether a divorce was friendly or bitter. A healthy man will at some point decide to move on, to start anew. While divorced men in their twenties and thirties usually aim to get back their old single life, divorced men in their forties and fifties want to start over.

The biggest and most often contemplated change is a career change. Sometimes this is very positive; other times it's foolish. Men often ask the women they date what they think of the changes they plan to make, and women tell them the truth. Women in their forties and fifties are far more honest than they were when they were in their twenties; they no longer feel obliged to tell little lies to protect the man's ego. But tread carefully: Men who find themselves suddenly single after forty are often lost. In an attempt to feel younger, they may lose weight, update their wardrobes and hairstyles, or learn a few new dance steps. If you shoot holes in a divorced man's dreams, he'll run away as fast as he can, because he thinks of his former wife as someone who held him back. His way of protecting his ego is to say, *Who needs her?*

This doesn't mean that if you're serious about a man you should applaud his plan to chuck his career as a neurosurgeon and start a rock-and-roll band. But don't tell him he's a fool for thinking about it, either. You can discourage him diplomatically without shooting him down.

The second message you want to send is, *I am friendly.* The easiest way to send that message is by smiling. The big, broad smile we advised against for women in their twenties, however, is even worse for a woman over forty. Both men and women over forty with broad smiles are seen as phonies. After forty a repressed smile or looking as if you might be about to smile works, while a broad grin doesn't. The good news is that most women reading this book who are in their forties, fifties, or sixties understand that they shouldn't be grinning all over the place as if they were twenty, and they don't. But 10 percent of the over-forty women we met did smile and giggle too much and acted as if they were still in their twenties. It turned off most men. It has the same effect as wearing a miniskirt when you're too old for one. No matter how terrific you think your legs are, don't do it! Most men have a sense of what is appropriate, and most are repelled by forty-plus women who try to look twenty. Smile, but keep it low-key.

Getting to Know Someone Over Forty

In your twenties or early thirties, getting to know the other person usually takes place slowly. Most young couples spend four or five dates determining whether the other person meets their expectations. When couples are over forty, they get to know each other much more quickly. This is because they go on the type of dates where they exchange information. This often fools women; they think the relationship is developing more rapidly than it really is. The fact that a man tells a woman about his life and his tastes and inquires about hers within two or three weeks of their first meeting doesn't mean he is any more committed than a twenty-year-old who has been dating for the same amount of time. In fact, both men and women over forty are much more reluctant to commit emotionally to a relationship than they were at twenty-something. So although there is an acceleration in exchange of information, there is often a slowdown in emotional commitment. Older men and women are leery about members of the opposite sex. Almost all of them have had at least one or more negative experiences. Many of them have been hurt before, and they do not want to be hurt again.

After you know enough about a man to consider having a serious relationship with him, the most important message for you to send is that you aren't going to hurt him. Don't use subtle hints; they won't register with most men. You almost have to tell men straight out that you aren't going to hurt them, although you can't put it in exactly those words.

Vera is a wonderful example of this. She told us that the minute she and her future husband became serious, she made him sit down and describe the people with whom he worked and how he thought she should treat each one. She knew how important his career was to him, and she wanted to reassure him that she would work at being a perfect corporate wife. When we spoke to him separately, he told us that this was exactly what she had done. From that moment on, he knew that he could count on her to be supportive.

Mary was more direct. She told Ted, whose previous girl-friend had broken up with him two months before they were to be married, that she loved him and would never leave him. When we interviewed them separately, both remembered her saying that and said it changed the nature of their relationship.

Although verbal assurances are important, men over forty in most cases are not going to be convinced your intentions are good just by what you say. You have to back up your words with deeds. Acts of kindness are very important. It is critical that you be kind and considerate when dealing with men over forty. Take into account their feelings and their needs and show them you care for them. When you were in your twenties, you told people how much you cared. Now that you are in your forties, fifties, and sixties, you must show people as well as tell them.

Many of the signposts that a relationship is on its way to being serious no longer have the significance they had when you were younger. When you reached the comfortable stage in your twenties and thirties and you became a monogamous couple, that was a positive sign. The interesting thing about couples over forty is they often reach the monogamous stage shortly after their first date. It is not that they are committed to one person; it's simply that they do not have the opportunities young people have to meet members of the opposite sex. They're less likely to go to singles bars, dances, or similar gatherings, so many are monogamous before they are committed.

When you're over forty, monogamy is no longer one of the hallmarks of a serious relationship. Nevertheless, you should insist on it before you let him come to your place, take off his shoes, and get too comfortable with you. If you find out he's dating others, drop him. A large number of men in the forty-plus category find it easy to get comfortable with women because they have no intention of committing to any one woman, and they are always dating several.

Interestingly, when we looked at men in their sixties and seventies who were dating, we discovered that more of them had two or three girlfriends than men in their twenties, thirties, and forties. We found that while women in their twenties and thirties would not put up with such behavior, women in their sixties and seventies often did. When we asked those women why they tolerated it, they said there weren't that many sixty- or seventy-year-old men available. Nevertheless, if you run across one of these men at any age, you're wasting your time if you want to get married. He is unlikely to marry you or anyone else. He simply wants to sow and resow his wild oats.

Still, reaching the comfortable stage after forty is important. It normally occurs after two months in mature relationships. The only stage that is meaningful for forty-plus couples, however, is committed couplehood. It is only at this point that you can tell if anything real is going on. Men can very easily get into the comfortable and monogamous stage without being seriously committed. In couplehood, they put their partner above family members and friends. Your only problem is that it may be difficult to test his commitment if he's over forty. Many men over forty have just a few friends, and their families don't even try to tell them how to run their lives. As you might expect, if a man is forty, even if he was a Mama's boy at twenty, he has become independent.

By the way, if you find a man in his forties still living with his mother, he probably will never marry. Don't waste your time. The only exceptions we found were men who were recently divorced and had moved in with parents until they got their own place.

People at any age cannot be considered a couple unless they become confidants. They must feel free to share the most intimate details of their lives without fear that what they say will go beyond the two of them. But there is one very important exception to this rule. Even if he spends much of his time telling you what a bitch his former wife was, you cannot ask or expect him to discuss details of his past marriage. Remember that at one time he and his former wife were confidants, and he has the right to respect that confidence. If you try to force him to discuss some aspect of his past relationships, he may refuse. This doesn't mean he doesn't love you, or that he's not committed to you, or that he isn't serious about you. It's just that there is a part of his life he considers private, and you must respect that.

Some men discuss everything with their partners, and others do not. We met several men who broke up with women because the women insisted they discuss details of their past they considered personal.

Timing

Timing is much different when you are over forty. Even if you reach the critical stage of mutual sacrifice in three or four months—and often older couples do—it's probably too soon to try to get him to commit to marriage. Wait until you have been dating between six and nine months, unless you receive strong signals that he doesn't want to wait.

Older Stringers

It's even more important for you than for a twenty-year-old to make sure the man you're dating is not a stringer. If he's had serious relationships with a number of women before or after forty, tell him up front you expect a marriage proposal within a reasonable period of time. If he runs for the hills, you haven't lost much. The greatest obstacle to women over forty marrying is men over forty who don't have a clear understanding that a relationship is intended to lead to marriage.

A number of men and women over forty have no intention of ever marrying—or remarrying. If you tell one of these people at the beginning of a relationship that you're looking to marry, many will call it quits. Still, you're better off risking it than spending a year or two dating them with no result.

Remember, for any woman at any age, wasting time can be a fatal mistake—it can kill your chances of marrying. While I advise women in their twenties and thirties not to bring up the subject of marriage too early in the relationship, I advise women over forty, once a relationship becomes comfortable, to drop none-too-subtle hints about marriage.

Two Points of View

We ran two focus groups with engaged men over forty who told us that within the last four years, they'd had a long-term relationship with a woman other than the one they were marrying. We eliminated from the group the men who said their fiancée was much more attractive than the woman they did not marry, even if they claimed that was not the reason they had chosen her. The first group was directed by a male researcher and the second by a female researcher. Each researcher wrote an independent report, but we videotaped both sessions so that after completing their reports, each had an opportunity to review and comment on the other session. We were looking for male and female perspectives, and we received them.

The male researcher reported that these over-forty men chose women who treated them with kindness and affection. They gave specific examples demonstrating the differences between the way the two groups of women treated the men they were dating. The women the men married were more affectionate. They not only kissed and hugged more often, they had sex more often—and, according to their partners, seemed to enjoy it more. In addition, the women the men married went out of their way to please their partners. They cooked them their favorite meals and kept a supply of their favorite beverage on hand.

The female researcher reported many of the same facts, but her follow-up questions and her interpretation of the data were different. She also reported that the men in her group said the women they were going to marry were more affectionate. As with the first group, they hugged, kissed, and made love more willingly and more often. But she also reported that they spent more time snuggling and touching because the women insisted, and the women about to marry also insisted that their men be more romantic. They pressured their partners to take them to dinner and shows, while the women the men did not marry were more often satisfied to sit at home with the men and watch TV.

> *Although the women the men were going to marry did treat their men with kindness and did on occasion cook their favorite meals or serve them breakfast in bed, most insisted upon and received reciprocal treatment.*

For example, the men bought flowers for the women they eventually married twice as often as they did for the women they did not.

Both researchers agreed that the couples who married seemed to act younger than those who broke up. The male researcher put it best when he said the couples who married acted more like twenty-four than forty-four or fifty-four. The researchers also agreed that the men and women who were about to marry had more fun together. The male researcher

noted that this was in part because the women in the successful relationships insisted they do more youthful and entertaining things. Both researchers said the successful couples
were more romantic because the women insisted on it, and in
the long run that helped those relationships.

Finally, the researchers recommended that women over
forty insist on romance both because they will enjoy it and
because it can lead to love and marriage.

Statistical Truths: If You're Looking to Marry After Forty . . .

> ➤ The best places to meet eligible men when you are over
> forty are clubs and groups—recreational, athletic, or
> based on other common interests. Join organizations
> that have single men as members.

> ➤ You are more likely to marry over forty if you have
> an active social life.

> ➤ Don't judge a man solely by his social skills—give
> yourself a chance to get to know him and give him an
> opportunity to improve his social graces.

> ➤ Be sure your own manners and social graces get high
> scores.

> ➤ Men over forty marry women who take care of them-
> selves, so it pays to stay in shape, dress well, and be
> meticulously groomed.

> ➤ Acts of kindness attract men over forty.

> ➤ When you and your man are over forty, it is impera-
> tive that you talk openly about money.

➤ Make a good first impression—no matter what your age.

➤ Delay him, do not dump him, if he comes on too strong too soon.

➤ If you're a religious person, have faith. Men who attend places of worship are more likely to marry.

➤ Insist on romance—it often leads to the altar.

7

Widowed and Divorced Men: Handle with Care

WITH AMERICA'S very high divorce rate, a substantial percentage of women who get married will wed a man who has been married before. While on the surface the relationships that lead to these marriages seem to follow familiar paths, they are actually very different. The primary reason for these differences is that men who have been married usually come to new relationships with financial obligations, emotional baggage, or children. Any one of these, and certainly various combinations of the three, will modify the nature of most relationships.

Financial Obligations

We interviewed hundreds of women who were marrying men who had been married before. Only about 30 percent of them had a real understanding of their future husband's financial obligations to his first wife. When the subject was raised with these couples in focus groups, many of the women were startled by what they heard. In the chapter on marrying after forty, I described how men often attempt to explain their financial obligations before getting into a relationship, and how some women refuse to talk about the subject. I'm not sure why some women react this way; it's risky and shortsighted. My first recommendation is that before you get involved in a serious relationship with a divorced man, find out exactly what obligations he has as a result of his earlier marriage or marriages. If he doesn't ask you about your finances, you should certainly ask him about his! If you marry him, his obligations will affect you, your children, and any children you might have together.

Remarriage

The factor that determines whether or not men who have been married before will remarry is the relationship they had with their previous wives. These relationships often leave men with heavy, messy emotional baggage, which they lug into all subsequent relationships.

Widowers

Although all men who have been married before have some baggage, its nature and impact are dramatically different between men who are widowed and those who are divorced. The basic difference between the two groups is that widowed men often have the emotional baggage of a fond attachment to the late wife, whereas divorced men often have a bitter or an antagonistic attitude toward the former wife. Widowers, if marriage has been a positive experience for them, are much more favorably disposed toward remarriage than are divorced men.

Widowers Without Children

Widowers without children are the most marriageable men on earth.

Ninety-one percent of those we interviewed were favorably disposed toward marriage, and because they had lived with a woman for years, they were comfortable with the idea of being married. Young widowers are much more skillful with women than the average single man. If they set out to charm a woman, they are very often successful. After living comfortably with a partner, these men are at ease with women and know exactly what to say and what buttons to push. Once they start dating, they're quick to marry. If you find one you like, don't waste any time—chances are he won't be on the loose for long.

Young Widowers

Widowers without children and younger than forty-four are the group most likely to marry; the only question is when.

Widowers Over Forty-Four

Most widowers between forty-four and forty-eight would like to remarry. In fact, many of them marry sooner than younger widowers because they are less likely to have toddlers. Their problem is meeting eligible women; they're too old for the singles scene. As a result, although most of them would like to marry, they often do not. Those who do usually meet their brides through work.

The next group is widowers between ages forty-eight and fifty-six. They are also likely to remarry, and when they reach fifty-two, the chances that they will remarry do not drop significantly. In general, the younger a widower is, the more likely he is to remarry, and the older he gets, the less likely he is to remarry. Until widowers reach fifty-six, remarriage is a common goal. For some reason, around that age they stop actively pursuing the goal. Still, if they meet the right woman under the right circumstances, even after that age, they will marry. The idea of marriage will appeal to them, especially if they were happy in their marriage.

Once widowers have gone through the grieving process, they are more likely to remarry than divorced men the same age.

The Two-Year Rule

It is usually not advisable to start a relationship with a widower until his wife has been gone a year and a half to two years. The reason is very simple. It usually takes men this amount of time to complete the grieving process and get used to dating again. It is thus wiser not to date a man whose wife passed on less than two years ago.

When a healthy man who is used to living with a woman finds himself alone and sexually frustrated, he seeks the companionship of a woman. Many of these men use prostitutes, including men who have never been with a prostitute before in their life. A number of them told us basically the same story: After having sex with women for whom they had no feelings for about a year, they decided to date someone they might like. While they didn't feel guilty about sleeping with women they didn't care about, as soon as they went out on a "real date," they were racked with guilt or overcome with grief, because the potential for emotional commitment brought back memories of their departed wife. This killed most of these relationships. A number of very sophisticated men told us stories of dates they had six months to a year after their wife died that turned into disasters.

The classic example was that of a very macho marine, Bill, whose wife had passed away very suddenly. At first he was in shock, but after three or four months he found himself sexually frustrated and lonely. Since Bill was stationed in a country where prostitution was readily available, he started going to prostitutes. A year later he was shipped back to the States, and after he'd been at his new post only a couple of days, an old friend's wife set him up with a woman she knew. Bill didn't want to visit prostitutes anymore, so he liked the idea. He took this very nice woman to a very nice restaurant. Three years later, Bill still doesn't know what brought it on, but in the middle of the meal he started weeping uncontrollably. He was embarrassed, and he pulled himself together long enough for the woman to leave quietly, but he knew she never wanted to see him again. Bill's only comment was, "Thank God I wasn't wearing my uniform." He went home and did not date again for more than a year.

Other Factors

Another factor that can have a significant impact on whether a widower will remarry is how his wife died. Often men don't want to discuss this; it's painful and makes them uncomfortable. If they talk about it without giving any details, however, it's a red flag.

This is particularly true if the man is over forty-four, but it's true for all widowers.

If his wife died of an agonizing disease, or if she lingered and he was her primary caretaker, the widower is much less likely to remarry.

When we spoke to such men, particularly when they were over fifty, a majority said they had no intentions of marrying again, and most gave the same reason: They didn't need another woman to take care of. They spoke as if that were the only relationship they could have with a woman. Some of them had taken care of their wives while they were ill for as long as ten years, and to them that came to define their marriage. When we pointed out to them that women generally live longer than men and usually end up taking care of their husbands, it made no difference.

A typical example was John, who worked in the post office in a small town. He started work at 8 A.M. and at lunch went home and fed his wife, Helen, who was bedridden. John returned at three in the afternoon and made her a cup of tea. Since it was a small town where everyone, including the postmaster, knew about his wife's illness, John was assigned to a route near his home so he could drop in during the day. At night, he prepared dinner for the two of them and took care of her needs. John did this for more than twelve years. He loved his wife and had no regrets, but he said he would not even consider remarrying. He was a member of a focus group made up of widowers from various backgrounds. When he told the other widowers how he felt, they all reassured him that most women don't need to be nursed. He simply shut his mind to their arguments. He refused to discuss the subject; in fact, he insisted he couldn't discuss it. After a few minutes the other men backed off, understanding that he couldn't handle the idea of having a relationship with a woman. Obviously, John was not ready to remarry.

A similar group of widowers were those whose wives died very painful deaths, particularly of cancer. They discussed at length how their wives had suffered and how painful the memory was. They were very reluctant to make another emotional commitment. One fellow, Ed, who had fought in Vietnam, said, "It's like being in a rifle platoon. For new men, it's the loneliest place in the world." He went on to explain that in a rifle platoon, when a new man arrives no one talks to him, no one wants to know him, because nobody wants to have to feel the emotional loss if he gets killed. Ed said he had the same reaction to women. He didn't want to get emotionally involved because he didn't think he could stand seeing someone he loved die that way again. Ed worked in the medical field and understood that the odds of the situation recurring with another woman were remote, but that made no difference. The emotional reality of his life was that he could not bring himself to take the chance.

Ed and John both had women with whom they slept. We spoke to the women. Ed's friend said she understood that he didn't want to get married, and she was happy with that. (One of the truths about women over forty who have been married is that a substantial percentage of them are not eager to remarry. In fact, in many relationships between people over forty, the man is more likely to push for marriage than the woman. My female researchers came to the conclusion that marriage is a better deal for men than for women, and I agree.) The woman seeing John knew he didn't want to marry, but she hoped to change his mind. There's a possibility she will, but it's doubtful.

At least these two women understood the reasons for the men's unwillingness to commit. We ran across many women who were dating widowers and didn't realize that these men would never marry again. They had never considered inquiring about how the first wife died. A number of men we interviewed said they would not discuss their wives' death with anyone. It was a particularly painful subject, even when she had died peacefully.

You cannot insist, but you can usually get this information by talking to a man's friends or relatives. It's very important information to know before you become too serious about someone with such resistance to marrying again.

Meeting at Work

Interestingly, when we spoke to widowers coming out of marriage license bureaus, we found a substantially higher percentage of them had met the woman they were marrying at work than any other group of men. I suspect this is because they have so little opportunity to socialize that they seek relationships wherever they can find them. If you would consider marrying a widower, looking around your company might be very productive.

Divorced Men

By far the largest group of available men, as you get older, are divorced. Before describing how different types of divorce affect men, I must tell you that I am giving the male perspective. I'm sure that in all divorces there are two sides to the story, and that many women reading this book will think focusing on the male side is unfair. But if you are looking to, or are willing to, marry a divorced man, being aware of how they think will give you an edge.

Amicable Divorce

The first type of divorced man is a rarity: the man who has had an amicable divorce. Most often the couple got married when they were very young and mutually decided they did not belong together. The older couples in this group agreed together to go their separate ways. In 90 percent of the cases, these couples don't have children, and their marriages were short-lived.

Divorced men of this type are very likely to remarry, because marriage was not a painful or unpleasant experience; it was more like one long unsuccessful date. They'll tell you that getting divorced was emotionally draining, and it may have cost them something financially. Nevertheless, they don't have hostile or negative feelings toward their ex-wives or women in general.

This is not normally how divorced men feel. For the overwhelming majority, *amicable divorce* is an oxymoron.

The Low-Hostility Divorce

The second type of divorce is low hostility. When these marriages end, there are hard feelings and usually bitter words. No matter what caused the breakup, there tend to be acrimony and accusations. But after some time has elapsed, divorces in which all they fought over was who was most at fault often turn into low-hostility divorces. Couples who disagreed about money or other things but left the fighting to their lawyers and never really got personally involved often have low-hostility divorces. Men from these relationships are likely to remarry. Similarly, men who were divorced in the distant past, or are the type who do not hold grudges, are apt to remarry.

Divorce is a nonissue when a man does not love his ex-wife, hate his ex-wife, or even think about his ex-wife. From his perspective, they've gone their separate ways, and that's that. Men who think this way are also very likely to remarry. Like most divorced men, they have great skills with women and are used to being married. They often remarry within a year or two of their divorce.

Divorce That Is Amicable on the Surface

A majority of the divorced men we interviewed told us their divorce was the common garden variety: nothing special. When we interviewed these men, however, we discovered several varieties of the "common divorce."

When a couple get divorced, both parties are usually bitter, and the experience is anything but pleasant. But when both partners, in the best interests of the children, declare a truce even before the ink on the divorce papers is dry or shortly thereafter, the man is immediately a good candidate for re-marriage. Couples like this are at least amicable on the surface. The wife doesn't tell the children that the father is a loser, and he doesn't imply that his wife is a miserable hag. They try to support each other as much as they can when making decisions concerning the children. As a result of this mutual interest, they actually develop a mutual respect for each other. If this goes on for a while, it develops either into an operating truce or a limited but amicable relationship. Sometimes they even become friends. Their outlook is: *We were lousy as a cou-*

ple, but we're good as parents. Men who have this type of relationship respect their ex-wives and other women and are very likely to remarry.

The Almost-Amicable Divorce

The man and woman who have an almost-amicable divorce cooperate in some ways on raising the children. The men pay child support and sometimes alimony, and both parties are relatively satisfied with the arrangement. Usually the man thinks he's paying too much and the woman thinks she's being paid too little, but both live with it. The man may occasionally be late with payments or do something else that drives his ex-wife crazy. The woman may have her lawyer send her ex-husband threatening letters or give him a hard time when he arrives to pick up the kids. They do not, however, involve the children in their fights. They put the children's interests first, and as a result have a standing truce.

After several years, men with this type of relationship with their ex-wives are likely to remarry, because once again marriage has not been a totally negative experience for them. Even though divorce is usually marked with acrimony, after a while the bitterness dissolves.

The Minimally Cooperative Divorce

Both parties in these divorces claim they put the children first, but they do not cooperate with each other. Usually, one or both is still very angry and finds it almost impossible to successfully mask his or her feelings, even in front of the children. The woman will allow the man to see his children, but she gives him a hard time when he shows up. She thinks the children need a father, and although she detests her ex, she puts up with him. He has a similar attitude toward her. He thinks she is petty and mean, but she *is* the mother of his children, and he puts up with her. There is a thin veneer of amicability over their mutual antagonism, but they try to keep the veneer intact for the sake of the children. Men in this type of relationship with their ex-wives may remarry only after they have been divorced a while.

When the antagonism comes closer to the surface, however, the chances either party will remarry drop sharply. If one or both parents make snide remarks about the other to the children, it raises the antagonism to a new level. Most divorced parents compete for their children's affections in some way. Men often buy bigger and better gifts or spend more money on the children than they should, while the women become superdoting mothers. Such competition affects the chance of a man remarrying only when it goes too far and he and his ex-wife stop talking to each other.

> *When a man maintains an ongoing relationship with his ex-wife for the sake of the children, even though it is not amicable on the surface, he is more likely to remarry than one who breaks off communication altogether.*

Of course, communication is not necessary if there is no reason to communicate. If there are no children or mutual interests, such as a business, they need not talk and, in fact, probably should not be talking.

Bitter Divorces

And then there's the bitter divorce. The man believes he got taken; he's convinced his lawyer lost the case and that he's paying a lot more than he should. He thinks he's a victim of the system. Divorced men in this group are often bitter about the settlement. If it drives them crazy for only one or two years, it is not uncommon for them to remarry. But if after five or six years they are still railing against their ex-wives, they are not likely to remarry—nor would they be a good candidate for marriage.

Least Likely to Marry

We found that men whose wives had walked out on them, cheated on them, or treated them badly in other ways were seldom eager to remarry.

Men who have been treated terribly or betrayed by their wives are not likely to marry again. This is particularly true if their wives embarrassed or humiliated them. You should avoid men who have been emotionally destroyed by their ex-wives as well as men who are in ongoing battles with them. Most will never remarry.

There are several ways of identifying these men:

➤ The first is they actively and passionately hate their wives long after the divorce. They are constantly talking about their ex's actions as if they were still married.

➤ The second characteristic of divorced men who are not likely to remarry is that they have limited contact with their children because their ex-wives make it difficult for them to get together.

These men clearly have an ongoing antagonistic relationship with their ex-wives. No matter who is at fault, these men are unlikely to marry. Any continuing conflict with their exes reduces the likelihood men will remarry, and if the conflict is over seeing their children, the chances are reduced even more. Avoid these men—they would not make good husband material even if they did want to remarry.

We also found divorced men who will probably never marry because they no longer trust women.

Men whose ex-wives have used their children as a weapon against them very seldom remarry.

Most commonly the ex-wife deliberately obstructs the development of a relationship between young children and their father, or if the children are older, severs whatever relationship already exists. I interviewed a number of divorce lawyers while preparing this chapter, and they agreed that some wives have legitimate reasons for not wanting their ex-husbands to see the children, but others withhold the children as punishment. Most men become very bitter if they believe their wives have turned their children against them by accusing the men of abuse or worse. Regardless of whether the accusations are true, these men hate their ex-wives and do not trust women. Avoid these unsuitable suitors.

Those divorced men who are convinced they were cheated in the divorce and have made up their minds not to pay are unlikely to remarry.

Some from that point on dedicate their lives to beating the system.

We interviewed men who quit high-paying positions and were working at menial jobs to avoid paying child support or alimony. Rather than give their wives money, they do without themselves. One man who was an advertising executive was working as a night clerk in a flophouse hotel. This man, along with several others who took menial jobs, was well educated, articulate, and clever. I do not understand this group of men, but they exist, and the chances they will remarry are almost nil. Again, avoid these unmarriageable men.

Single Fathers with Children

When you first talk to single fathers, they may seem unmarriageable, but they are not. With special handling, they are excellent candidates for marriage.

When a widowed or divorced man has the sole or primary responsibility for raising his children, this fact usually dominates his life. No matter who watches their children during the day, the vast majority of single fathers are obliged to take care of the house and the children at night and on weekends. In most cases, they find this an overwhelming burden. We had two single mothers interview these men because we thought they would have some idea of what they were facing. Before interviewing widowers and divorced men with children, these women were convinced single fathers had it easier than single mothers. After the interviews, however, they came to the conclusion that many were in a much more difficult position than women. Single mothers are seldom overwhelmed by having to do something for which they're unprepared. When they come home from work at night they're exhausted, but they know how to care for children and manage a home. The men they interviewed did not fare nearly as well.

One of the female researchers concluded that single mothers had fewer problems than single fathers. Her research partner did not agree, but admitted she wasn't sure which group faced the greater difficulties. Both researchers were surprised at how inept men were at handling ordinary chores. After running several focus groups with single fathers, they discovered that after a year many did not know how to clean a house, when to do the laundry, what to buy at the grocery store, what food staples to keep on hand, or even how to buy clothing for children.

According to these interviews, it took most men two years to master running the house, and some never seemed to get the hang of it. After two years or more, one in three of the men were still running to the store several times a week more than necessary, doing things two or three times, and generally working harder than they should while getting less done. They told our researchers that they regularly sent their children to school wearing clothing they'd worn the day before.

Fathers find it easier to raise sons than daughters, and they usually do fairly well handling one child. When they have several children, particularly very young ones, the fathers find themselves in over their heads. The two single mothers who did the interviews found that in some ways the men were in the same position as some single mothers. When they come home from work, they face another eight-hour workday. At the end of the evening, they fall into bed exhausted, then drag themselves out of bed an hour early the next day so they can prepare breakfast and get the kids off to school or day care. Most days are carbon copies of the day before. On the weekend, they can't sleep in because there's a long list of household chores to be done. They have little or no time, energy, or opportunity for a social life.

Single Fathers

For discussion's sake, we divided single fathers into groups. The first is fathers with preschool children. These men are almost always overwhelmed by responsibilities for which a man's life has not prepared them.

Their situation is particularly unfortunate if they don't have family support. If their mother or an aunt takes care of the children while they work, they are much more likely to remarry than if they're on their own. When they have to hire people to take care of their children, however—particularly if this leaves them financially strapped—their chances of remarrying are slim.

The second group is single men who have children in school. Most of them have a schedule similar to women with preschool children, but most single fathers whose children are of school age arrange to have someone take care of their children after school. Children who go to school do not need their diapers changed or to be fed every couple of hours and are generally easier to manage. Most of these fathers soon learn to prepare meals and help their children get ready for school. Their lives are hectic and exhausting, but about 60 percent try to arrange their time so they can have some kind of a social life.

Children

The next stumbling block for women who date divorced or widowed men are the men's children. They mainly fall into two categories: children who live with the father, and children who stay with the father on weekends and other occasions. The first group of children represent a far more significant problem than the second. No matter how antagonistic children who live with their mothers are toward you, they're with their father only for short stretches of time and therefore have limited influence. In addition, they realize you won't have much impact on their lives, so you're a minor threat. Children living with their fathers, in contrast, can be a real obstacle. Though the information presented below applies to both situations, the scenario is much, much worse if the children are living with their father full time.

Teenage daughters often become jealous, controlling, and possessive of their fathers once their dads start to date. Even younger girls can be protective and competitive. This type of opposition is usually easily handled.

The main fear children have when their father brings a new woman into their lives is that they are going to lose their dad. They've already lost their mother, either through divorce or death, and they're terrified of another loss. The father must prepare them by assuring them, and then reassuring them, that they aren't going to be loved less or get less of his attention when a new person comes into his life. He needs to make them understand that love is not something that can be divided, but can be multiplied. Children learn best through examples they can relate to and understand. He can explain that parents with six children love each child as much as parents with two children love each of theirs. They don't divide their love six ways so that each child only gets one-sixth of their love. Each of the children gets all the love either parent can give, and each of them will get all his love. If they can grasp this, they'll be more likely to accept a new person in their lives.

Another reason children resist someone new coming into their father's home is that they are, like most of us, apprehensive about change. They have questions. What will happen if a new person lives with us? What will she be like? What will she demand? Will she give me orders? How will she treat me?

After consulting with you, he should be the one to answer most of their questions. He should tell them enough to allay their fears without being absolute. He must leave wiggle room so he can change his mind if necessary. He should qualify his statements with phrases such as *I imagine; I don't think; under normal circumstances; in most cases; unless a special circumstance arises.* If the children want more definite answers, he needs to explain to them that he can't foresee every situation that may arise in the future, and these answers are the best he can give.

Most couples who have successfully brought children into their relationship have taken two steps. They arranged for the initial meetings with the children to take place in a location that was fun for the children, such as a ball game or the mall or a local amusement park. It's best to take children to places where they can't help but enjoy themselves. During the first few meetings, the father should carry on almost as if the new person weren't there. The woman should appreciate but not intrude on their fun. If the woman comes on too strong too early, it often alienates the children. They want someone who won't bother them, who isn't going to upset the balance they're used to, and initially that's what you have to give them. If during the early meetings you seem too loving or too eager to please, you will turn off most children.

Ideally, these first few meetings should be nonevents as far as the woman's presence is concerned; there shouldn't be any pressure on the children or on the woman to interact. This is the "let them get used to the new person" stage—nothing more.

After several outings in which the children have limited interaction with the woman, it's time to progress to the second stage, which is to get the children used to her in a normal environment. If the father—prior to the new relationship—usually buys pizza and ice cream and watches a movie with the kids, that should be just what happens, the only difference being that you're there, too. Sit on the couch next to him while he's watching the movie, but don't get too affectionate. Afterward, everybody does their dishes just as they did before you arrived. The normal routine has to remain intact. Remember, you want to convince the children that nothing much is going to change. Once they feel secure that you're not going to upset their lives, that things will go on as before, they'll start to relax. Whether you're with them for the weekend or all the time, keep it low-key.

Next, you should attempt to do fun things with the children, but only if they want to do them. If the kids would like to go to a soccer game or a football game but their father won't be available, you can offer to take them. Once again, the ideal interaction should have the informality of an ordinary day. Whether you take a teenage girl shopping at the mall or a small child to the zoo for just an hour, the object is to let them get used to being with you. Do something they want to do, do something they enjoy, and be very pleasant.

This is a gradual process. It takes time. Don't rush it. Your primary goal is to reassure the children you aren't going to change their lives.

Finally, there are a few things the successful couples we interviewed advise against:

> ➤ If the father has the children on the weekend and the son or daughter has a soccer game, go to the soccer game. Don't make the child give up the soccer game because you made plans to do something else.

➤ Don't force kids to give up a game, a Girl Scout meeting, or music lessons. Let them do the activities they
normally do. Reassure them, through your actions, that
their lives will go on, that there will simply be another
person there who is very pleasant and supportive.
Remember, tread carefully—they can stop a marriage
before it starts.

➤ On the other hand, you should never put up with a
child who is rude or antagonistic. The father must tell
the child that he or she doesn't have the right to pick the
father's friends. No matter how badly the child behaves,
as long as the fight is between the father and the child
or children, the adult should eventually win.

➤ Women should avoid being drawn into an argument
with a man's children. If a child challenges or is rude
to you when the father isn't present, you must let him
or her know the behavior is not acceptable and that
you're going to report it to the father.

Eventually, you'll have to be able to control the children
when you are the only adult present. The first time you tell
children to do something they don't want to do, they'll probably tell you that you are not their mother and have no right to
give orders. Do not let that stand. Start by agreeing that you
are not their mother, and add that you don't have any intention of trying to take their mother's place. However, since
you—like their teachers in school—have been put in charge
by their father, you have not only a right but a duty to demand
minimum standards of behavior. "Unlike your mother, both
the teachers and I can be overruled by your father. You have
every right to complain to your father about any orders I give

you, but you don't have the right to defy me. If you think you do, we'll need to have a discussion with your father." Your primary goal is avoid a one-on-one confrontation with a man's children.

I ran a focus group with six engaged or married couples who had children from previous relationships. They were very helpful. At the end of the session, when I asked them if they had anything they wanted to tell couples facing these challenges, they said to be patient, support each other, and get away from the kids when they begin to get to you—which they will. Finally, they wished you good luck. You'll need it.

Statistical Truths on the Delicate Dance with Divorced and Widowed Men

➤ Divorced and widowed men often carry a lot of bulky, messy emotional baggage—identify it before you take on a load you'd rather not carry.

➤ A divorced man's financial obligations can impoverish the woman who marries him.

➤ Young widowers without children are the most marriageable men on earth.

➤ Single fathers with children have little or no time or energy for a social life.

➤ Most widowers are not ready for a serious relationship until at least a year and a half to two years after their wife passed away.

➤ How a man's wife died can affect his attitude toward marriage.

- One of the best places to meet a widower is in the workplace.
- The more amicable a man's divorce, the more likely he is to remarry.
- The younger a man is, the more likely he is to remarry.
- Once a man's children are convinced their lives will not be disrupted by their dad's new love interest, they'll feel less threatened and will be less antagonistic.
- Nothing happens overnight. Be patient.

8

Meeting Online

W E PLACED THIS chapter to follow those on marrying after forty and marrying widowers and divorced men because many singles in these categories are meeting online. Although most using the Internet are somewhat older, the cyberspace singles scene is becoming more and more popular, and it seems destined to become a standard dating tool.

Once again, because we're dealing with human beings, developing statistically valid information does not automatically create valid advice. For example, when we started in the late 1980s, less than 1 percent of the engaged couples we interviewed met through personal ads or a dating service. By 1998, more engaged couples met online than through traditional personal ads and dating services combined. By 2000, approximately 3 percent of the couples we met coming out of marriage license bureaus had met online, and their numbers were growing, particularly among the forty-plus age group.

You might then expect that a book designed to help women marry would tell every woman over forty to get online immediately, but it isn't that simple.

After talking to several hundred women who had used personal ads, dating services, and online chat rooms to meet men, as well as law enforcement officers and people who ran dating services, we came to several conclusions.

> First, women *are* going to use all these services.
> Second, use of the Internet by women seeking men is growing and will probably continue to grow.
> Third, for women with limited social contacts, particularly those too old for the singles scene, it is their best and in some cases their only way of meeting eligible men.
> Fourth, meeting a strange man can be dangerous—but there are ways of protecting yourself.

Safety First

For safety's sake, give out as little personal information as possible before you meet. Women with computer savvy set up a special account to use online dating services. If you are not sure how to do this, ask a friend who is familiar with the Internet or ask your Internet company for help.

When you meet a man through personal ads, a dating service, or online, always arrange to meet in person for the first time in a public place, preferably where there are people who know you. The best place is a restaurant or coffeehouse. Never let him pick you up at home or at work.

If at any time during a date you get a bad feeling about the man, get away or into a well-lit public place immediately. Don't worry about embarrassing him or embarrassing yourself, and do not delay. The only rape victim I interviewed was picked up at work in a car by a man she had arranged a date with. She felt something was wrong almost immediately and thought about jumping out of the car when he stopped at a red light, but she was too embarrassed. She's wished every night since that she'd followed her instincts.

I also spoke to two detectives; both said many victims of violence have a feeling that something bad is going to happen but are too embarrassed to act on their feelings. If you get a bad feeling, act on it, and act immediately.

If you do not have a cell phone, get one and bring it with you. You can always call for help or a taxi.

It's generally a good idea to exchange pictures before you meet. This serves three purposes. Men who use these forums to take advantage of women don't like to send pictures, so if he's hesitant to send a picture along, beware! If he dates only women who look like reed-thin models, and you're built like Mae West, both of you are wasting your time. Finally, if he doesn't look like his picture, he is lying or has something to hide. Do not date him.

Don't assume, as many women do, that because you have talked to him on the telephone several times, you know him. Some men who are charming on the phone are anything but in person.

Red Flags

Still, I am not suggesting that you *not* use the telephone to screen your dates—it can be very useful. Ask as many questions as you can on the phone, and don't date anyone who sounds as if he's being evasive.

If he pays for everything in cash, not just on one date but all the time, that's a red flag. Married men usually don't use their credit cards when they're playing around; they're afraid their wives will see the credit card statement and question them. If he pays cash, tell him you've heard that about one-third of the men meeting women through personals or the Internet are married, and they usually pay cash. If he denies being married, ask to see his wallet. If he is telling you the truth, he probably won't object.

When they're caught, most married men feign innocence and indignantly storm off. Some, however, become belligerent and intimidating. If that happens, call the police and have them escort you to your car or a cab. They'll be happy to do it. In the past, when a woman suspected a man was married, she asked him for his home phone number. Now that cell phones have become commonplace, that no longer works. Still, it remains a good idea to ask a man for his phone number when you meet online and to insist on calling before you meet him in person.

Private Detectives

The most effective way of checking on a man is to use a private investigator or one of the online background checking services, which cost about $75 to $150. I recommend one or the other if you suspect that he is married, or is not who he says he is, or if you have a feeling something's not right. If he travels a distance to meet you, if you met as a result of an ad or online, or if he asks you to make an emotional or financial commitment soon after meeting you, it might be time to hire a professional to look into his background. One detective I interviewed said, "If he seems to be too good to be true, he just may be." Confidence men are very charming and tell women exactly what they want to hear. The detective's comment was: "If he isn't worth a background check, he isn't worth dating."

Apparently, many women agree, because these checks— which at a minimum tell you if he is married or has a criminal record—are often used today, not only by women who have substantial personal wealth but also by those who, after a couple of dates, still know little or nothing about the man they are dating. I met four women planning their weddings who said they had used a private detective to check out their future husbands, and only one told him she had done so. Three of the women had met their future husbands online, while the fourth went through a dating service. Three out of four had checked out men before they met their fiancés. They all agreed that it was a good idea to check on a man if you met him on the Internet or through the personals.

The woman who met her fiancé through a dating service said she did her own checking there as well. Her dating service required everyone who joined to sign a document allowing the firm to check the truthfulness of the application they filled out. But she discovered, after speaking to a woman who worked for a dating service, that the services very seldom, if ever, checked on anyone, so she went to a detective agency. When the agency reported that he was married, she decided to check on anyone she met through the dating service. The next one she met, she checked immediately.

He was her fiancé when we met. She claimed checking on him had helped their relationship develop more smoothly. She said it was easy to trust him about his feelings once she found out he was being truthful about his life. Two of these women had dumped men they had checked on because of what they learned. The first was a married man signed up with a dating service, and the second had been arrested three times for drunken driving. Three of four women said that now that they knew how easy it was, they thought it would be a good idea to check on any man who seems like a good prospect before you become seriously involved.

Most women do not use a private investigator to check on their dates—in fact, only a small percentage do. Still, almost one-third of the women who used the Net to meet men told me that they had run across one or more married men pretending to be single; a few of them wasted months dating these men before finding out they were married. These women thought hiring a private investigator was a great idea. And so do I.

Reach Out Online, but Remember . . .

➤ Meeting men online, through personal ads, or through a dating service is often effective, but it can be dangerous.

➤ Don't believe that because you have talked to a man on the telephone, you know him.

➤ For safety's sake, meet only in public places, tell a friend where you're going, take your cell phone, and have your own transportation.

➤ If a man seems like a good prospect but you have some doubts, get a background check on him.

Conclusion:
Defending Marriage

On two occasions when I spoke on the subject of why men marry I was accused of being a male chauvinist. The women who attacked me claimed: I was feeding into the myth that it was women who wanted to marry. That marriage was a male institution designed to control and/or take advantage of women. That marriage benefited women more than men. Or that marriage was the only or at least the best way for people to form meaningful relationships. None of which they thought was true.

I told those who thought men desire marriage as much as women to look around and count the number of men in the audience. It was obvious that this was a subject in which large numbers of women and few men had an interest.

I then pointed out that the idea that marriage was an institution designed to control women was already seen as a myth in the tenth century. A very entertaining tour guide in London told of a monk who, while copying an ancient manuscript on marriage, noted in the margin that marrying couples was like putting them on a horse. While the man usually sat up front and held the reins and looked as if he controlled the speed and direction of the horse, it was often not so. Some strong women made the man ride behind from the beginning. Other strong women allowed their husbands to sit up front and hold the reins, yet made every decision. But even very feminine and seemingly weak women, who encouraged the husband to be in control, whispered in his ear whenever they came to an important crossroad and had more to say about the couple's final destination than the man. If a monk understood the true nature of marriage a thousand years ago, we should today.

While I did not maintain that marriage benefited women more than men, I did point out that it protects them and their children in the legal system if the relationship fails. In some states women are entitled to half the property that was earned during the time of the marriage; in the others the man has some responsibility for supporting both the women and any children after a divorce. Women who live with men without marriage find it much more difficult to make such claims.

While researching this book, we ran across dozens of women who lived with men for decades and thought they had no need of a marriage license. A number of them found out the hard way that they did. These women could not even visit their dying partners in the hospital, because they were not related. Some were kept out by a wife who had not seen the man in years, and others by children who were raised by the man's ex-wife. They moved in and claimed estates these mistaken women had helped build and thought were theirs.

There are many reasons to marry, but the most important is that marriage dramatically increases the chances the relationship will last. While half of all marriages end in divorce, by my estimate fewer than 5 percent of other living arrangements last a lifetime.

Finally, children from homes with two parents do better in school and in life than those raised under other circumstances.

If you are a woman who wants a traditional marriage with husband and children, do not let anyone talk you out of your dream. It is not only romantic—it is also very practical.